Self-Discipline and Mental Toughness Mindset

Achieve Your Goals and Success, Daily Habits and Exercises to Become Productive, Develop an Unbeatable Mind, Iron Will, and Confidence

Stephen Patterson

© Copyright 2019 - All rights reserved.

The content contained within this book may not be reproduced, duplicated or transmitted without direct written permission from the author or the publisher.

Under no circumstances will any blame or legal responsibility be held against the publisher, or author, for any damages, reparation, or monetary loss due to the information contained within this book. Either directly or indirectly.

Legal Notice:
This book is copyright protected. This book is only for personal use. You cannot amend, distribute, sell, use, quote or paraphrase any part, or the content within this book, without the consent of the author or publisher.

Disclaimer Notice:

Please note the information contained within this document is for educational and entertainment purposes only. All effort has been executed to present accurate, up to date, and reliable, complete information. No warranties of any kind are declared or implied. Readers acknowledge that the author is not engaging in the rendering of legal, financial, medical or professional advice. The content within this book has been derived from various sources. Please consult a licensed professional before attempting any techniques outlined in this book.

By reading this document, the reader agrees that under no circumstances is the author responsible for any losses, direct or indirect, which are incurred as a result of the use of information contained within this document, including, but not limited to, — errors, omissions, or inaccuracies.

Contents

Self-Discipline 1

Introduction 3

Chapter 1:
The Power of Willpower 5

Chapter 2:
Human Behavior and Self-Discipline 16

Chapter 3:
Motivation 45

Chapter 4:
Facing Failure 58

Chapter 5:
Developing Good Habit Fundamentals 68

Chapter 6:
Vocabulary for Success 81

Chapter 7:
Strategies for Self-Discipline 96

Chapter 8:
Controlling Your Environment 100

Chapter 9:
Develop Drive _____ 105

Chapter 10:
Directing Your Attention _____ 109

Chapter 11:
Social Motivation _____ 115

Chapter 12:
Measuring Progress _____ 121

Chapter 13:
Don't Weigh Pros and Cons _____ 126

Chapter 14:
Keeping Your End in Mind _____ 129

Conclusion _____ 132

Mental Toughness Mindset _____ 133

Introduction _____ 135

Chapter 1:
Discover the Champion Mindset _____ 136

Chapter 2:
Improve Your Self-Confidence _____ 143

Chapter 3:
Improve Your Self-Discipline _____ 153

Chapter 4:
Improve Your Attitude _____ 163

Chapter 5:
Improve Your Control of Negative Emotions _____ 172

Chapter 6:
Improve Your Leadership Skills _____ 182

Chapter 7:
Improve Your Emotional Intelligence _____ 190

Chapter 8:
Improve Your Ability to Remain in Control _____ 200

Chapter 9:
Improve Your Ability to Trust Your Instincts _____ 209

Chapter 10:
Improve Your Mental Fortitude _____ 217

Chapter 11:
Improve Your Assertiveness _____ 227

Chapter 12:
Improve Your Ability to Set Goals Successfully _____ 236

Conclusion _____ 244

Self-Discipline

Blueprint to Success in 10 Days for Entrepreneurs, Weight loss and Overcome Procrastination, Laziness, Addiction - Achieve Any Goal with Powerful Long-Term Daily Habits and Exercises

Stephen Patterson

SELF DISCIPLINE

Blueprint to Success in 10 Days for Entrepreneurs, Weight loss and Overcome Procrastination, Laziness, Addiction - Achieve Any Goal with Powerful Long Term Daily Habits and Exercises

Stephen Patterson

Introduction

Willpower is a person's ability to control their desires, attention, and emotions. People have started to realize that willpower plays a vital role in their success in every aspect of their life. Everybody understands that they are supposed to have control over every area of their life, but a lot of people feel that they are failing at that.

The American Psychological Association believes that a lack of willpower is the main reason why people struggle to reach their goals. A lot of people feel guilty if they let others or themselves down. Others are at the mercy of their own cravings, thoughts, and emotions. They live their lives based on impulses and not conscious decisions. Even people that have their life together end up feeling exhausted at holding everything together, and they start to wonder if things are really supposed to be so hard.

Willpower and self-discipline are what helps people feel in control of their life without feeling stressed about it. This isn't something you can develop overnight. It will likely take you quite a while before you completely understand what it means to be disciplined. But it can be done, and you can do it.

In this book, you will find information about building daily self-discipline that can be used in all areas of your life. This book is about turning you into a person that is disciplined every day, and you will be able to successfully use this for growth. Besides learning how to become more self-disciplined, we will also look at different ways to become stronger mentally. It can sometimes feel hard to have to push through those obstacles, especially if you don't think you have enough willpower, but this book will provide you the tools you need to knock over those obstacles and keep going.

Chapter 1:
The Power of Willpower

Everybody mostly thinks that their life can be improved if they had a bit more of the mysterious thing known as willpower. With a little bit more self-control everybody could stop procrastinating, save for retirement, avoid drugs, stop drinking, exercise more, and eat right. The American Psychological Association performs an annual Stress in America Survey. They ask their participants, among several other things, about their ability to make reasonable changes in life. Their number one reason for not following through with changes is lack of willpower.

While most people blame a lack of willpower for their problems, they have not entirely given up hope. Most people who responded to the survey felt that they could learn willpower. They could be right. Research has recently found ways that willpower can be strengthened. But there were survey participants that felt that more time for themselves would improve their willpower. That is probably not going to help them out anyway. Scientists, over the past few years, have made some discoveries about how willpower works.

Willpower is not the only reason why a person may not reach their goals. Roy Baumeister, Ph.D. and psychologist described three critical components for achieving a person's objectives. First, you need motivation for the change and a clear goal. Second, your behavior needs to be monitored toward the goal. The third is willpower. No matter if your goal is to spend less time on social media, study more, kick a bad habit or lose weight, willpower is an integral part of achieving your goal.

Willpower basically can resist short-term temptations so that you can reach long-term goals. There are many different names that we give willpower: self-control, self-discipline, resolve, drive, and determination. In psychological terms, willpower tends to be defined as:

- A limited ability that could be depleted.

- Conscious regulation of the self that takes effort.

- Being able to use a "cool" cognitive behavior system instead of a "hot" emotional system.

- The ability to be able to override unwanted impulses, thoughts or feelings.

Self-Discipline

- Having the ability to delay gratification and resist temptations to reach long-term goals.

One hundred thousand years ago, for people to survive, they had to find food, avoid predators, and reproduce. Being a part of a tribe increased their odds of survival. Taking somebody else's girlfriend or dinner could jeopardize their lives, but also the life of the tribe. Self-control was essential for survival back then and played an important part in evolution.

Willpower is already present in all of us since we were born, but not many can use it effectively. An efficient and straightforward test was conducted by a psychologist, Walter Michel, to determine the willpower amongst children. It is called the marshmallow test.

A plate of marshmallow was presented by Michel's team to the preschoolers. The children were informed that they would be left alone for a few minutes and if they were able to wait until the researcher came back in, the child would get two marshmallows. If the children decided to ring a bell to bring immediately back the researcher because they couldn't wait any longer, they would only be given one marshmallow.

Thirty years after the initial test, the team followed up with the children. They have observed that the children that waited for the second marshmallow have been living a better life and have high scores on SATs and lower BMI. Self-control has proven to be a good indicator of academic achievement over intelligence, a better determinant of good leadership over charisma, and is more critical for marital satisfaction over empathy. People that have more willpower tend to be:

- Healthier

- Happier

- Have better relationships

- Make more money and better off in their careers

- Can manage stress better and deal with conflict

Neuroanatomy

The prefrontal cortex is located just behind the forehead and eyes, and it controls our behavior, thoughts, and abstract thinking. This means that it helps in mediating conflicting ideas, enables you to make choices between right and wrong, and predict the outcome. Naturally, it controls the things that we pay attention to, thinks about, and feel.

Self-Discipline

The prefrontal cortex has grown significantly during human evolution, which tells us that there was an intense selection pressure that helped it to grow and evolve. Let's put this into perspective. The last five million years has increased the brain about three-fold. At the same time, about six-fold has been grown by the prefrontal cortex.

The prefrontal cortex is the last part of the brain to mature. The development of this part is likely to be finished when it reached approximately 25 years old. This is probably the reason why sensible and intelligent teens take part in excessive or high-risk behaviors even though they know the possible outcome.

To help you understand the importance of the prefrontal cortex for willpower, let's look at what can happen when it's damaged. Phineas Gage's story is a prime example. In 1848, at 25 years old, Phineas Gage was working on the rails as a foreman. He was a well-respected man and considered to be respectful and quiet. His physician said that he was active both physically and mentally.

Unfortunately, something went wrong when he was working a routine procedure on September 13. A tamping iron with the length of seven inches has pierced through Phineas' skull and somehow damaged his prefrontal cortex. Surprisingly, though, he didn't die and made a full recovery in a few months. However, something was not right and very different, although his wounds have healed. His friends and colleagues have observed the change in his personality. Dr. Harlow, his physician, said this about his change:

"The balance between his intellectual faculties and his animal propensities seems to have been destroyed. He is fitful, irreverent, indulging at times (...) impatient of restraint or advice when it conflicts with his desires..." It is said that he lost his willpower when he lost his prefrontal cortex. There are still more things that can damage the prefrontal cortex aside from accidents such as this. Being distracted, sleep-deprived or drunk can leave us less equipped to help with our impulses. If the prefrontal cortex controls how we question whether we need an expensive pair of shoes, then what controls our impulses and cravings? It is said that on our minds, two people are living. This is based on some neuroscientists.

There is the good one who takes the long-term goals into their account, and the other one is the spoiled one who wants instant gratification. Everybody has both, and we switch between the two from time to time. The primitive brain is what neuroscientists call the area of the brain that is in control of our desires and cravings. The hippocampus, hypothalamus, and amygdala can be found on the primitive brain. This area controls your long-term memory, motivation, behavior, and emotions.

When a willpower challenge happens, like with the marshmallow example, the primitive mind will scream for that candy, but then the prefrontal cortex jumps in and reminds us that we would prefer two pieces of candy.

Willpower is in a constant clash between these two systems. Walter Michel, the researcher behind the marshmallow study, created a framework they referred to as the "hot-and-cool" system that explains how willpower will either fail or succeed. Your cognitive and thinking system is called the cooling system while your impulsive and emotional part is the host system. The hot system controls the responses to specific triggers.

Strengthening Your Self-Control
There has been much research conducted over the recent years that have looked to explain all the different facets of willpower. Most researchers who explore self-control have the same goal in mind: How can we make willpower stronger? If willpower really is a limited resource, as other research has suggested, what can you do to conserve it?

Staying away from temptation is one great way to maintain self-control. In the marshmallow study performed by Walter Michel, the children who sat and stared at their treat was a lot less likely to resist that treat than the children who shut their eyes, looked away or found a way to distract themselves. This "out of sight, out of mind" idea also works for adults. One study was able to discover that office workers who had candy in the desk were less likely to indulge than if they placed their candy on their counter where they could see it.

Another good way to help improve self-control is what psychologists refer to as "implementation intention." Typically, these intentions will take the form of "if-then" statements that will allow people to be able to plan for moments that could end up foiling their resolve. For example, if a person is watching their alcohol intake, they may tell their self before going to a party, "If somebody offers me an alcoholic beverage, then I will ask for club soda with lemon." Research that looked at adults and adolescents found that implementation intentions can improve self-control, even for people who have had their willpower depleted by lab tasks. Coming up with a plan of time could end up allowing you to decide within the moment without having to use your willpower.

The research that suggests that we might possess a limited amount of willpower causes a few troubling questions to come up. If we are faced with a lot of temptations, are we going to fail? Not necessarily. Researchers don't think that a person's willpower can ever be entirely used up. Instead, people appear to keep hold of a reserve of willpower that they can use for future demands. With the right motivation, we can tap into those willpower reserves, which will allow us to persevere even if out self-control has been run down.

Mark Morven demonstrated this idea and found that willpower-depleted people were able to persist on self-control tasks when they knew that they would benefit other people or be paid for the efforts they exerted. This means that high motivation could help a person overcome weak willpower, at least to a certain extent.

Willpower may be less vulnerable to depletion. Researchers who have studied self-control have described willpower as a muscle that can become fatigue when used a lot. But there is another part to the muscle analogy. While muscles do become exhausted, they will strengthen when regularly used over the long term. This means that periodically exerting self-control could end up improving the strength of your willpower.

Morven and his colleagues, in one of their first demonstrations, asked participants to follow a two-week regimen of tracking their food consumption to help their posture and mood. When compared to the control group, the people who exerted more self-control by doing their assigned exercises were not as likely to experience willpower depletion in the follow-up tests.

In another one of his studies, he discovered that smokers who used willpower for two weeks by staying away from sweets or regularly using handgrips ending up being more successful. The successful participants gave up smoking while control subjects who went on two weeks performing regular tasks that didn't require self-control on their part, like writing in a journal did not.

Other people have also been able to prove that flexing your self-control muscle can strengthen the willpower with time. Australian scientists Ken Cheng Ph.D. and Megan Oaten Ph.D. of Macquarie University in Sydney gave participants a two-month exercise program, which was a routine that would require them to use willpower. At the end of the program, the participants who were able to stick to their plan ended up doing better on the lab follow up of self-control than the other participants that didn't get assigned an exercise regimen. That's not the only thing either. The participants also said that they smoked less and drank less alcohol, ate healthier foods, monitored their money spending, and improved their study habits. Working their self-control while working out led them to have better self-control in almost every area of their life.

With the discoveries that suggest willpower depletion is connected to the glucose levels, they tell us that there may be another remedy. Eating regularly so that the blood-sugar levels in the brain are maintained could help to refuel willpower. Dieters who aim to keep their willpower without reducing calories may do better when you eat frequent small meals instead of skipping lunch or breakfast.

All the evidence from the willpower-depletion studies has also shown us that creating a long list of resolutions on New Year's Eve is probably the worst thing you can do. Being depleted in an area can lower your willpower in other areas, so it only makes sense that you should concentrate on just one goal in a single time. That means, don't try to start an exercise program, adopt a healthy diet, and quit smoking all at one go. It's best to take your goals in a one by one approach. After you have gotten a good habit in place, you will no longer have to draw on your willpower to keep performing this behavior. Eventually, following healthy habits will be your normal routine, and you won't have to decide at all.

Chapter 2:
Human Behavior and Self-Discipline

Self-control is what separates us from our ancestors and the rest of the animal kingdom. As you know, this comes from the prefrontal cortex of the brain. There is of debate within the science field as to whether willpower is a finite resource. This is what is known as ego depletion.

Some studies have found that exercising willpower requires a lot of mental energy, especially on the reserves of glucose, which is the fuel the brain prefers. This all can lead to depletion or weakened willpower. The central concept of this ego depletion is one reason why people are more apt to grab a cookie when they feel stressed out and not when they feel on top of the world.

Recently, though, scientists have been unsuccessful in replicating some of the studies that underlie ego depletion. There is more research underway, but the verdict on if you can "run out" of willpower remains to be seen.

Self-Discipline

If you remember the marshmallow study from the last chapter, the results seemed to indicate that willpower is an innate ability, but reviews, later, suggest that our willpower changes over our lives and it can be improved with practice. Having a better understanding of why we tend to cave to some impulses, but we can resist others, is crucial for obtaining an understanding of eating disorders, impulsivity, and addictive behaviors.

Whether you find that you are most tempted by scrolling through Facebook, sex, food or drugs, we all have different areas in life where we could use a little bit more willpower. There are ways to strengthen your willpower, which is what you will learn throughout this book. Some of the most common ways to increase willpower are through mindfulness, routines, and rewards. Strengthening willpower isn't always easy, but the benefits can improve your quality of life, work performance, and health. We're going to look at how willpower affects different bad habits and how you can work through these habits.

Procrastination

Procrastination is something that we all face at some time in our life. For as long as humans have existed, we've had to struggle with avoiding, delaying, and procrastinating on things that matter. While we are productive when we have figured out how to not procrastinate, we feel accomplished and satisfied.

Alright, let's figure out what procrastination is. Procrastination is such a timeless problem. The term Akrasia was even created by Socrates and Aristotle to describe this behavior. When you act against your better judgment, you can call it Akrasia. Even though you know that you should be doing something different and may be important, you still do something else.

It's great to have a definition, but why do people procrastinate? Behavioral psychology has found what is known as "time inconsistency," which explains why we all fall prey to procrastination even though we have good intentions. The tendency of the brain to value immediate results more than future rewards is what is known as time inconsistency.

Think about it this way. You have two selves: The Present Self and Future Self. When you create goals, such as learning a language, losing weight or writing a book, these are your Future Self's goals. You are trying to prepare yourself on want you want in your life in the future. When you think about the Future Self, as scientists have discovered, the brain will notice the value in taking actions easier with long-term benefits. These long-term rewards are what the Future Self likes.

However, the only one that can act is the Present Self, no matter how the Future Self loves these goals. Your Future Self is no longer there when you decide. Since you are now situated in the present time, the Present Self is now what the brain is concentrating on. Scientists have found that the Present Self does not like much the long-term rewards compared to instant gratifications.

This puts the Future and Present Self at odds a lot. While the Future Self likes to be trim and fit, the Present Self says otherwise and wants to eat a donut. Everybody knows that they need to eat healthy now so that they don't wind up overweight ten years down the road, but risks like heart failure and diabetes are still far away.

Similarly, no matter how well most young people know it is essential to save money for their retirement when they are still young, they again can't act because they feel that the payoff is still decades away. Instead of saving the money they used to buy expensive shoes for the future, the Present Self even purchases the shoes anyway.

Therefore, you still go back to old patterns in the morning, even though you feel motivated to change your habits before you go to bed the night before. When the rewards are set to happen in the future, the brain prefers these long-term benefits. However, when the mind is in the future, it prefers immediate gratification. Keeping your Present Self-motivated cannot rely on consequences and long-term rewards. It's important, instead, to figure out how to move the rewards and punishments to the present. The future results must be made as present consequences.

An important note about the action line is that as soon as you are over that line, your pain will start to go away. In fact, staying in the middle of procrastination tends to be more painful than being in the middle of the work. The anxiety, guilt, and shame that you experience while you are procrastinating tend to be worse than the energy and effort that you must put into the actual work. The problem lies in starting the job, not doing it.

There are many ways that you can stop procrastinating.

Make Your Reward for Action Immediately.

If you can make it seem that the benefits of your long-term decisions are immediate, procrastination can be much easily avoided. One great way to do this is to use a strategy known as temptation bundling.

Katy Milkman came up with temptation bundling through behavioral economics. This strategy suggests that you bundle an excellent behavior in the long-term along with good practice in the short-term. Some good ways to bundle temptation are:

- When you have monthly meetings, you can prefer to only hold it on one favorite restaurant.

- Only enjoy your favorite show while you do chores or iron.

- While processing work emails, you can get a pedicure.

- You can exercise and listen to audiobooks at the same time.

The Consequences Should Be Made Immediately

There are several ways to make you forcefully face the consequences of your procrastination right now instead of later. For example, you can exercise with your friend so you will be compelled to work out and not be a jerk if you miss one out. This is much better than just working out alone where you may tend to be lazy and not exercise at all.

Create Your Future Actions

A favorite of psychologists is to use a "commitment device." These will create, ahead of time, a future action. One example would be to buy food that is individually packed instead of buying things in bulk to help curb your eating habits. You can also remove your applications and games on your cell phone so you will not waste time. These are just some of the many ways on how commitment devices can help reduce procrastination.

Create Achievable Tasks

The thing with procrastination is that it is hard to start the behavior or even change the current one. Reducing the size of the habits is a good idea because it will be easier to start when they are smaller. By these, it will make you procrastinate less.

A great way to make a habit easier is with the two-minute rule. This rule says that "When you start a new habit, it should take less than two minutes to do." The goal is to make it much easier for you so you can quickly get things started and trust that you can finish the task through the momentum. It will be a lot easier to continue a job when you start performing it. That's why the 2-minute rule helps you to overcome laziness and procrastination by making tasks much more accessible to begin so you don't have the time to say no.

Along the same lines, you can break your tasks into smaller sections. Take, for example, Anthony Trollope. He has published two plays, 12 short stories, 18 works of non-fiction, 47 novels, and several letters and articles. How was he able to achieve this? Instead of looking at his progress through finished books or chapters, he

Self-Discipline

looked at his development in a fifteen-minute time span. His goal is that within 15 minutes, he should write 250 words. He continued this every day for three hours. This way, he felt satisfied and accomplished every fifteen minutes, while he was working towards the goal of finishing a book. So, we've looked at beating procrastination daily. Now, we need to make this productivity a habit that will last for a long time and prevent procrastination from returning.

We slip back into procrastination because no system will determine what needs to be finished first and what is essential. The best productivity system we are going to look at is called The Ivy Lee Method:

- At the end of the day, write out six things that you need to get done tomorrow. Only six, no more than that.

- Prioritize the six things in order of real importance.

- The next day, focus on the first thing on your list. Work until you have finished that first task before you start the second one.

- The remaining items on your list should be worked in the same way. When you have unfinished items on the list after the day ended, those items should be moved back to the top list for the following day.

- This should be repeated daily.

This is a great way to get started beating that procrastination habit. You can only make willpower work for you if actual start working.

Addiction

Addiction can be classified as a person engaging in behavior or the use of a substance where the reward provides them with a compelling incentive to repeat the action despite the possible negative consequences. Addiction can involve things like nicotine, cocaine, opioids, inhalants, alcohol, or behaviors like video games or gambling. Scientific evidence shows that addictive behaviors and substances share key neurobiological features; they activate intense brain pathways of reinforcement reward, many of which involve dopamine.

Addictive behaviors tend to be accompanied by mental health conditions like anxiety and depression or other pre-existing issues. These addictive behaviors not only use a lot of the same brain mechanisms of compulsivity, but they also respond to similar treatments.

Self-Discipline

There isn't a single cause of addiction, although biological factors like genetics could contribute to the vulnerability to the problem. Many environmental, social, and psychological factors influence substance use as well. There isn't a single personality type that can be associated with addiction. The only thing that can link to addiction is the ability to tolerate strong feelings like distress.

While all addictions tend to cause a sense of hopelessness and feelings of failure, as well as guilt and shame, research has found that recovery is the rule and not the exception and that there are several different routes to recovery. This road to recovery isn't going to be straight: relapse or recurrence of use is very common, but it does not mean it's the end of the road. For people who can achieve remission for five years has the likelihood of relapse that isn't any greater than the general population. To diagnose an addiction, their need to be at least two of the following things present in the person:

- The activity or substance is used in large quantities or for a period longer than was intended.

- There is a want to reduce use or unsuccessful efforts to do so.

- The pursuit of the activity or substance or recovery from it takes up a lot of time.

- They have a strong desire or craving to perform the activity or use the substance.

- The activity or substance use disrupts obligations at home, work or school.

- Their activity or substance use continues despite their interpersonal or social problems that it creates.

- Participation in important recreational, social or work activities stops or drops.

- Use tends to happen in situations where it is risky.

- Use will continue despite knowing its cause or exacerbates psychological or physical problems.

- Tolerance occurs. This is known either through a need to diminish the effect of the same amount or increase the amounts to achieve the desired result.

- Withdrawal happens and manifests either in the presence of withdrawal symptoms or the need to take something to block them.

The severity of the problem is gauged by how many symptoms are present. Two to three symptoms mean there is a mild problem. Four to five symptoms mean there is a moderate problem. Six or more symptoms indicate that the condition is severe. There are many different biological, environmental, and psychological factors that can contribute to a risk of addiction.

Scientists believe that genetic factors can contribute to about half of the risk of developing an addiction. There is a factor that links to vulnerability due to a variation in a gene that determines the brain's receptor makeup for dopamine. Another factor could be the nature of the hormonal response to stress.

Physiological factors can play a part in addiction. A variant in liver enzymes that metabolizes different substances could influence alcohol abuse.

Gender is also another big factor. Males tend to be more likely to develop substance abuse disorders, although this "gender gap" could be narrower for alcohol abuse, and females tend to be more prone to intoxication effects at a lower amount of alcohol.

A person that tends to be a sensation seeker and impulsive is at a higher risk of addiction. Impulsivity is mainly related to a risk of relapse.

A person who has suffered through trauma or abuse is also at higher risk. Perhaps, through sensitizing the brain pathways of distress and alarm due to the added burden of stress, early exposure to large amounts of adverse experience can contribute to developing a substance abuse disorder because the coping ability has been overwhelmed.

Mental health problems like PTSD, ADD, anxiety, and depression increase the risk of addiction.

A strong family relationship has been shown to reduce the risk of substance disorders, but many different aspects of family circumstances or functioning can contribute to a higher risk of addiction. If you have a sibling or parent with an addictive disorder, the risk higher, as does a lack of parental support or supervision. Troubled parent-child relationships and family disruptions increase risk. Research has found that marriage and child-raising responsibilities mitigate addiction risk.

If a person has easy access to alcohol or other substances in their home, at work or school, it increases a person's risk of repeated use. The people you hang out with also increases your risk of use. If you're around people who use, especially during the teenage years, you are more likely to develop an addiction.

Self-Discipline

Lastly, employment status plays a part. Having a job and growing your skill set exerts pressure for stability and provides you with psychological and financial rewards that help to mitigate the chance of addiction. While there are many different types of addictions out there, we're going to look at the three common addictions and how to overcome them. We won't go back through the symptoms because addiction symptoms are the same no matter the addiction.

Video Games

Overcoming a video game addiction, much like all other addiction, can be difficult. However, with enough time, a person can learn to enjoy playing video games without being addicted. The following tips could help a person overcome their addiction.

Do not quit cold turkey – Video games, unlike other addictions, take up a lot of time. Quitting altogether can leave a large space in a person's life, and can cause a person to relapse, sinking them further into their addiction. The goal should be to curtail the amount of time that is spent playing the games.

Moderation – Come up with a specific number of minutes or hours to play video games each day. Set a timer and when it goes off, stop playing.

Lower the number of systems in the house – Between handhelds and consoles and other gaming systems, you can't play all of them in a limited time. A lot of people try, though. Instead, reduce yourself to a single system that you play games on. This will let you focus on one system without feeling like you must play a game on each one of your systems.

Stay away from MMO's – MMO's are the worst games to play if you have a severe addiction. They waste a lot of time. Some people have even died while playing them since they tend to play for days at a time without taking a break.

Schedule breaks – For every hour you play, stop, stand up, and take a walk for a few minutes. It's not good to sit in front of your TV for long periods of time without a break.

Limit the amount of money you spend on games – Allow yourself $60 or less each month for video games. This means you should only be buying one or two games a month. Limiting your spending will limit your addiction.

Pick games that require physical activity – There are more and more games that are becoming movement based. There are some that require you to stand and move around. They may still be video games, but they do encourage exercise.

Self-Discipline

Make it a family thing – There are plenty of games out there that families can do together. This will let you play games while also spending time with family. Remember, though, that you should teach your children moderation. This could end up increasing an addiction, so it may not be the best option for you.

Get help – There could be some underlying issues as to why you're addicted to video games. Finding a mental health professional is a good idea and you should not be ashamed of it. A PCP could help you as well.

Figure out if you have other issues – Your video game addiction could be caused by some other problem in your life. Talking to a professional could help you find the other problem areas.

Pick up other hobbies – Create a collection, do gardening, and so on, just find something else that will keep your mind and hands busy. You can also include family and friends in some of these.

Review your life – Take a look at what your life is like right now. What areas could be better? Maybe you missed out on a job because of your addiction. You might have missed out on your child's school event. Try to right those wrongs.

If you still don't believe that video game addiction is real and is a big problem, let's look at the story of Shawn Woolley. In 2001, Shawn

Woolley killed himself. His mother found him and found that the online game Ever quest was running. The mother blamed the game for his suicide, but the Sony CEO disagreed.

There isn't any proof to whether Ever quest resulted in his suicide. His mother believed that his addiction to the game and his death could have been caused by a possible love interest in the game. Unfortunately, there isn't any real proof.

Addiction may have been a big part in Shawn's death. Shaw also suffered from physical and mental health issues, which were likely worsened by the fact that he was always in front of his computer. He had stopped working, stopped interacting with family, and stopped paying bills.

It's hard to say who is to blame. His mother tried to help, and it's not Sony's place to make sure that people get help. But this should be proof enough that video game addiction is a real problem.

Shawn's mother, in 2002, founded On-Line Gamers Anonymous to help other people who are addicted to video games. It's up to the family and friends to confront the addicted person about their problem. Everybody must help the addicted person to take responsibility. You can't just say, "It's only a video game."

Alcohol

First, think about these statements

- It's how I unwind and relax after a long day.

- I have fun drinking.

- It's how I forget my problems.

- I would have energy and time for activities and people that I care about.

- I would feel physically and mentally better.

- My relationships will likely improve.

- It affects my job performance and responsibilities to my family.

- I often feel ashamed, depressed, and anxious.

- It has created problems in my relationships.

Once you have decided to change, the next thing would be to come up to establish clear goals. The goals need to be clear, specific, and realistic. You do not want your goal to be simple, I will stop drinking alcohol. Instead, your drinking goals should look something like this:

- I will not drink on weekdays, beginning on (insert date).

- I am going to limit what I drink on the weekends to no more than three a day and five the entire weekend.

- After three months, I will reduce my weekend drinking to a max of two per day and three the entire weekend.

- It helps to answer these questions:

Are you interested in quitting altogether or cutting back? If you only want to cut back, you should decide which days you are going to drink and how much you will drink? What day do you want to quit drinking or start drinking less? Once you have set your goals, write down a few ideas on how you are going to accomplish those things like:

- Remove temptations from your office and home.

- Announce your plans. It's important for everybody you are close with to know what you are doing. You can even ask others who drink to not drink in front of you.

- Be truthful about your limit. Let people know if you are no longer allowing drinking to happen in your house and that you might not go to events that will have alcohol.

Self-Discipline

- Stay away from bad influences.

- Learn from your past.

Whether or not you are going to be able to cut back on your drinking successfully will depend on how severe your problem is. If you are an alcoholic, meaning that you have no control over your drinking, it is best if you quit drinking entirely.

Some people can stop drinking on their own or with a 12-step program or support group. Others will require medical supervision to withdraw comfortably and safely. Which way you choose will depend on how much you drink, how long you have been struggling, how stable your living situation is, and any other health problems you might have. There are four main alcoholic treatment programs:

- Residential treatment means that you will live at a facility while you undergo treatment during the day. These treatment programs typically last 30 to 90 days.

- Partial hospitalization is for those who will require ongoing medical monitoring but have a good living situation. These programs will typically meet at the hospital for three to five days each week and normally last four to six hours.

- Intensive outpatient programs work on relapse prevention and are often schedule around a person's school and work.

- Therapy can be used to help figure out the root cause of your alcohol abuse, fix your relationship, and learn about coping skills.

No magic treatment will work for everyone. Everybody is going to have different needs, so it is crucial you figure out the program that works best for you. With alcohol abuse, you will have to face withdrawal from alcohol. This is something that doesn't necessarily happen with video game addiction. When you have been drinking frequently and regularly for a long time, your body will become physically dependent on the alcohol and will go through withdrawal when you stop. The symptoms can include:

- Elevated blood pressure and heart rate

- Trouble concentrating or sleeping

- Stomach cramps and diarrhea

-

- Restlessness and anxiety

- Vomiting or nausea

- Sweating

- Shaking

- Headache

These symptoms will typically start within hours of your last drink and peak in one to two days, and usually improve after five. For some alcoholics, withdrawal can be life-threatening. If you have been a long-term heavy drinker, you might have to be medically supervised during your detox.

Drugs

Recovering from a drug addiction works a lot like an alcohol addiction. Your recovery from any addiction doesn't start by stopping your use. Instead, it is done by creating a new life where it's easier for you not to use. Everything in your life doesn't have to change, but there are some behaviors and things that have been causing you trouble. These things, if you don't let them go, will continue to get you into trouble. The more you try to retain your old life during recovery, the less well you will do.

You can use the same steps from the alcohol section to overcome drug addiction, but here are a few other things you can do.

Try to avoid high-risk situations. One easy way to figure out if you are in a high-risk condition is to remember the word, HALT: hungry, angry, lonely, and tired.

How are you feeling at the end of the day? You will probably be hungry if you haven't eaten well. You might be angry if you have had a tough day. You could feel lonely if you're isolated. You don't have to be alone to feel lonely. And you are tired. This is going to be when your strongest cravings occur. Other ways to know if you are in a high-risk situation are:

- If you are around people that you use to use with

- People whom you have conflicts with or people who encourage you to use.

- If you are in a place where you used to use.

- If you have things around you that remind you of using.

You can't altogether avoid these situations, but if you are aware of them, you won't be caught off guard. This will help you to prevent your cravings from turning into significant urges. Taking better

Self-Discipline

care of yourself will help. Make sure you have a healthy lunch, so you're not as hungry later. Join a 12-step program that you won't feel as isolated. Learn the best way to relax so that you can release your resentments and anger. Develop better sleeping habits.

People will withdraw from drugs just like they do from alcohol. The symptoms are all pretty much the same. Depending on your drug of choice and how long you have been using will affect your withdrawal symptoms.

Oversleeping

People often struggle to get enough sleep, so the issue of sleeping too much seems like a luxury. It's not. Just like insufficient sleep, oversleeping is a sign of disordered sleep. This problem could be connected to mental health. It could also mean that they have poor sleep quality, and a clinical sleep disorder could cause it.

Sleeping too much is also linked to many of the same health problems that are sleeping too little is related to, which includes cognitive issues, metabolic issues, and heart disease. People who sleep too much also have higher mortality risks. Hypersomnia is the clinical term for oversleeping, and excessive day sleepiness. Hypersomnia has a few core symptoms:

- Trouble concentrating

- Grogginess on and off through the day

- Trouble getting out of bed and beginning your day

- Difficulty getting up in the morning.

- Sleeping for longer periods of time at night.

Let's be clear that I am not talking about the once in a blue moon night of extra sleep. This can happen to everyone occasionally. If you keep your sleep routine consistent, it shouldn't happen that often. You're probably wondering how much too much sleep is. The tricky thing is that there isn't a single right amount of sleep for everybody. Rest is an individual need. The following are a few factors:

- Your genetics can influence your internal sleep drive and circadian rhythms.

- In your 20s, you may find that seven hours is enough, and you may need eight hours in your 50s or 60s.

- Sleep provides your body and mind with energy, so if you have exerted a lot of energy during the day, you will need more sleep.

- If you are working through health issues, you will probably need more rest. This is true for short-term and long-term conditions.

- Given your life circumstances, like periods of change or upheaval and stress, can temporarily increase your sleep need.

That said, most people during their adulthood will need somewhere between seven and nine hours of sleep. Some people may be good at six to six and a half hours, but it is improbable that you can function well at five hours of sleep or less. Similarly, some people need nine hours of sleep, but if you regularly sleep more than nine hours and you still wake up fatigued and tired, you could be oversleeping.

Teenagers and young adults will often oversleep as a sign of depression. It is difficult to gauge a teen's sleeping pattern because their sleeping habits are typically very different from adults. An estimated 40% or more people under 30 that suffer from depression will experience hypersomnia.

But, sleeping and depression have a complicated relationship. Disrupted sleep is a symptom of depression and a cause of depression. Most people that suffer from depression experience sleep disturbances. Sleep problems are also able to make depression more difficult and severe.

Sleep disorders aren't always seen as having a harder time sleeping. They can also interfere with the quality of sleep and can trigger oversleeping and excessive sleepiness. Any sleep disorder that causes sleep deprivation can cause excessive daytime sleepiness. Hypersomnia is closely linked to some specific sleep disorders:

- Narcolepsy is a neurologically based sleep disorder where the brain doesn't have any control over the sleep-wake cycle. People with narcolepsy tend to have excessive daytime sleepiness and strong urges to sleep. They will often have nighttime insomnia.

- Restless leg syndrome causes a creepy-crawly feeling in the legs. These feelings will often cause people to need to move their legs. RLS is normally more intense at night and often causes people to experience insomnia. These people will normally experience daytime sleepiness and could oversleep because they aren't getting enough quality rest.

- Obstructive sleep apnea compromises a person's breathing during sleep. While sleeping, the airway becomes completely or partially blocked for a short period of time. This will happen several times and can cause frequent awakenings.

- Idiopathic hypersomnia means that a person is excessively sleeping for no reason.

Substance abuse can also cause a person to oversleep, as well as other medical conditions like obesity, Alzheimer's disease, epilepsy, brain injuries, MS, and Parkinson's disease. If you think you have hypersomnia, you should talk to your doctor. It's also a good idea to limit your alcohol intake and do your best to avoid becoming sleep deprived.

No Motivation
You don't feel that much interested in doing extraordinary things when you have low motivation. No motivation happens when you aren't interested in doing anything. You start avoiding friends, decline or cancel social events, stop hitting the gym altogether, go to work only when you must, and you may self-sabotage.

Now, there are times when no motivation as usual. This happens when you go through a significant life change like bereavement, breakup, or redundancy. This is just when your mind needs a bit of a timeout. When no or low motivation has gone too far or may start endangering your life, it may become a mental health concern. Things to watch out for are:

- If it has gone on for over six weeks.

- If you don't know the reason why you don't be motivated.
- If you are experiencing suicidal thoughts.
- Is unchanged or worsened.
- If it is constantly accompanied by negative thoughts.
- If you start to lose interest in family and friends.

Considered as a big issue on mental health, depression can cause low motivation. Schizophrenia, acute stress reaction and bipolar disorder can also cause low motivation. If you are experiencing low motivation and you have an obvious trigger such as career issues or a life change, it is helpful to have self-help. If you cannot manage your low motivation anymore or it has already lasted long enough, it is now the time to talk to a coach or counselor.

Chapter 3: Motivation

Motivation is a mighty, yet tricky beast. Sometimes you may find that you get easily motivated, and you are wrapped up in a whirlwind of excitement. Then there are times when it is nearly impossible to figure out how you can get motivated and you feel trapped in a spiral of procrastination. This chapter will look at the best ways to get and stay motivated.

Don't worry, though, this isn't going to be some rah-rah pep speech. Instead, we are going to look at the science behind motivation and how you can keep yourself motivated. This could be figuring out how to motivate yourself or how you can motivate your team. Motivation is defined as a willingness to do something. It's a psychological force that compels you to perform some action. This is all science, but we can figure out a better definition of motivation.

Steven Press field, the author of The War of Art, described motivation as "At some point, the pain of not doing it becomes greater than the pain of doing it.". There will be a point where it is easier to change than to remain the same. It will be easier for you to act and feel insecure while you are working out at the gym than sitting still and experience self-loathing at home. It will become more comfortable for you to feel awkward while making sales calls than handling disappointed about your bank account.

This is the most basic definition of motivation. Every choice you make has a price, but when a person is motivated, it becomes easier to handle the inconvenience of the action than the pain you feel when you stay the same. Here's the vital question: what can we do so that we can make it more likely that we will pass that mental threshold and feel motivated consistently?

A surprising thing about motivation is that it tends to come after you begin a new behavior and not before. There's a common misconception that motivation comes because of passively consuming an inspirational book or a motivational video. However, active inspiration tends to be more powerful.

Motivation is typically a result of the action and not the cause of it. Getting things started, even if it's something small, is one form of active inspiration that will naturally provide you with momentum.

One great way of referring to this effect is the Physics of Productivity because it is merely Newton's First Law applied to habits:

objects that are in motion will stay in motion. After you have started a task, it will be easier to move forward.

Motivation isn't needed as much when you start a behavior. Almost all the friction with a task will start at the beginning. Once you have begun, your progress will happen naturally. Thus, a critical part of getting motivated is making things easy to start.

A lot of people will struggle to find the motivation to achieve their goal because they waste too much energy and time on other areas of their process. If you are looking to make it easy to find your motivation and get things started, then you need to automate the early parts of your behavior.

Something a lot of people tend to do to delay work is to start to think about when they are going to do it again. This can be seen with habits like creating art, starting a business, working out, and most other habits.

- If you don't have a set time for when your workout is supposed to happen, then you will wake up thinking, "I hope I have the motivation to exercise today."

- If you don't have a marketing system for your business, then you will show up with your fingers crossed that you will figure out how to get the word out, as well as everything else you must do.

- If you haven't picked a time to write something each week, then you will often find yourself saying something like, "I just need to a bit more willpower to get stuff done."

Creating a schedule seems relatively simple, but it will put your decision-making in autopilot by providing your goals a place and time to live. It will be more likely that you will follow through no matter how much motivation you have. Also, there is a lot of research that has been done on motivation and willpower to back this up.

Quit waiting for your inspiration or motivation to hit you and create a schedule for the habits you want. This is what separates the amateurs and the professionals. Professionals will design a program and stick to it. Rookies will wait around until they feel motivated or inspired.

How are some of the most prolific artists in the world motivated? They don't just create a schedule; they form a ritual. Twyla Tharp is one of the greatest choreographers and dancers of the modern era. In her book, The Creative Habit, Tharp talks about role rituals and how they have affected her success.

Self-Discipline

For example, in her book, she explains how she wakes up each morning at 5:30 AM, gets dressed for the gym, walks outside and hails a taxi, tells them to take her to Pumping Iron gym, and then she works out for two hours. Her ritual in this is not the weight training or stretching that she performs. Instead, her routine is hailing the cab and telling them where to go. This act stays the same for every day and habituative it and makes it less likely for her to skip her gym time.

Mason Currey, in his book Daily Rituals: How Artists Work, talks about how a lot of the world's great artists follow a regular schedule.

- Maya Angelou would rent a local hotel room and would go there to write. She would get there at 6:30 AM and would write until 2 PM. She would go home and edit it. She never stayed the night.

- Michael Chabon, a Pulitzer Prize winner, writes from 10 PM to 3 AM five nights a week.

- Haruki Murakami gets up at 4 AM, spends four hours writing, and then goes for a run.

The most creative people don't depend on inspiration or motivation. Instead, they follow a consistent routine and pattern. The following are some examples of how you could create a method and ritual to help with your motivation:

- Sleep better – Keep a "power down" routine that you perform before bed.

- Start every morning stress-free – Come up with a five-minute morning meditation.

- Be more creative – Keep a creative ritual that you do before you begin singing, writing, painting, or whatever it is you do.

- Exercise consistently – Do the exact same warm-up routine every day in the gym.

The power of your pre-game routine is that it will give you a mindless way to start your behavior. It will make starting your different habits a lot easier, and this means that following through consistently will be more comfortable.

The key to creating a good ritual is that it will get rid of the need to come up with a decision. What will I need to do first? When do I need to do it? How do I need to do it? A lot of people won't get started because they aren't able to decide how they can get started. You need your starting behavior to be automatic and secure so that you will have the strength to finish it when it ends up being challenging and difficult. To make motivation a habit, three simple steps can take to do just that:

- A good routine will begin by being so easy that you aren't able to say no. There should be no need to be motivated to start your ritual. For example, to get started writing, I will grab a glass of water. You could start your workout routine by putting on your running shoes. These are super easy tasks and there is no way you could say no. The most important part of all tasks is getting them started. If you aren't motivated at the start, then you are going to find that motivation will start after you have begun. This is the reason why a routine must be super easy to start.

- Your routine needs to get you headed towards your end goal. Having a lack of mental motivation is often connected with a lack of physical movement. Picture your physical state when you are unmotivated, depressed, or bored. You don't move all that much. You could be slumped on the couch. This opposite is true as well. If you make sure that you are physically engaged and moving, then you will feel energized and engaged.

For example, when you are dancing, it's hard not to feel energized, vibrant, and awake.

While you want your routine to be easy to start, it's important that you gradually transition into more physical movement. Your motivation and mind will follow that movement. It's also important to understand that physical activity doesn't always mean exercise. For example, if you want to get writing, your routine should bring you closer to writing.

You must stick to the same pattern every time. The main purpose of your ritual is to create several events that you will always do before you start a certain task. Your ritual lets your mind know, "This is what happens before I do (insert task)." Eventually, your ritual will become so close to your performance that by performing that ritual, your mental state will be primed. You don't have to know how to figure out your motivation, you only must start your ritual.

If you have ever heard of the 3 R's of habit formation: reminder, routine, reward, your ritual is nothing more than a reminder. Your ritual is meant to trigger your habit, even if you don't have any motivation for it. This is extremely important because when you don't have any motivation, it will often be too much work to figure out what you need to do. When you must face another decision, you will typically choose to quit. However, having a ritual will solve this

Self-Discipline

problem because you will know what you are supposed to do. You won't have to debate or decide. Lack of motivation won't matter. You follow your pattern. Here comes the critical part, learning how to stay motivated for the long run. We're going to do this with the Goldilocks rule.

Let's pretend that you're playing tennis. If you were to try to play a serious game against a child, you would soon find yourself bored. The match will be way too easy. But, if you were to try to play a game against a professional player like Serena Williams, Rafael Nadal, or Roger Federer, you will find that you are not motivated because it's too difficult.

Now, compare these two games with a game that you play against a person who is equal to you. As the game continues, you will make a few points and lose a few. You have a pretty good chance of winning, but only if you try. Your focus will narrow, and your distractions will disappear, and you will be invested entirely in the game. Your challenge will be "just manageable." Victory is possible but not guaranteed. Science has found that these tasks are more likely to keep you motivated.

Humans like to be challenged, but only if it is within their best zone of difficulty. Tasks that are under your abilities are boring, and functions that are beyond your abilities are discouraging. Tasks that are between the two are motivating. We want to be able to master a skill that is just beyond our current knowledge.

This is known as the Goldilocks rule. You want things that are just right. Working on tasks that fall under the Goldilocks rule is a key to maintaining your long-term motivation. If you discover that you feel unmotivated on a job, it is probably because it has floated into boredom or has become too complicated. You will have to figure out a way to pull that task back into your abilities where you feel challenged, but capable.

This exceptional blend of peak performance and happiness is often referred to as flow. Flow is what performers and athletes find when they find themselves "in the zone." This is a mental state where you are so focused on your task that everything else disappears. By following the Goldilocks rule, you will find yourself falling into the flow more often. But you will also need to measure your immediate progress. That means that measurement is an essential factor in motivation.

Hedonic Motivation
Hedonic motivation is the influences that come from a person's pain and pleasure receptors on their willingness to reach a goal or retreat from a threat. This is what is linked to traditional motivational

principles where people will avoid pain and learn toward pleasure. This is gained through acting on certain things that result from emotional and esthetic feelings like joy, love, fear, hate, and so on. According to hedonic principles, emotional experiences can be viewed as a gauge that can range from good to severe and the primary motivation is to try to keep the needle as close to the right side as possible.

For example, writing a report for work could have two types of motivators. One would be that you write a great story and get a raise, which is the pleasure. The second would be that you don't and get fired, which is the pain.

Historically, avoidance and approach have been linked to hedonic beliefs of pain and pleasure. Hedonic comes from a Greek word that means "sweet," which means "relating to or characterized by pleasure." This makes it interesting because while the hedonic motivation incorporates pursuing pleasure and avoiding pain, the concept is often linked to the positive connotation of pleasure. One example would be hedonic goods are often bought so that the person can find enjoyment and satisfaction in the item, and this experience is often seen as hedonic experiences. Pleasure and pain are the body's natural compass. They point us towards what needs to be done and will help us to figure out if what we are doing will help us survive.

As hedonic motivation became popular, so did other types of interpretations and views. Socrates was one of the first to start studying hedonic motivation. He felt that it was a person who should follow a specific course of action where pleasure would exceed pain, and if they didn't follow the said path, it would be because they don't understand what pain or pleasure could result.

Democritus viewed hedonic motivation a lot as Socrates did, but he never had a definition of what things were painful and what was pleasurable besides that people avoided pain and liked pleasure. He felt that each person knew what they wanted and what they didn't like.

Epicurus thought that with hedonic motivation, pleasure and pain would even out, and people would learn how they should do things in moderation. Later, philosophers also created their interpretations of hedonic motivation.

Thomas Hobbes' explained hedonic motivation as people will generally work to avoid painful or adverse environmental events and approach those that are pleasurable or positive, this is also known as

Self-Discipline

incentive motivation. Our learned remembrance on if something is unpleasant or pleasurable sets how we will approach an event.

Chapter 4:
Facing Failure

For those who haven't heard, "There's no such word as can't," I wonder how things would work if we all believed that statement, especially when it comes to going after our dreams. Think about all the excuses people make throughout the day and how they keep us from going anywhere:

- What will people think?

- I don't know if I'm ready.

- It's too personal to share.

- I'm not as good as (insert person).

- I can't write.

In fact, we are all already capable and competent. All you must do is accept it. Do you remember the story about the little engine that could? Once he switched up his mindset, he was able to change his destiny. You have the power to do the same.

Remember what Henry Ford said, "Whether you think you can, or you think you can't – you're right." You must begin believing that you are able to do anything, no matter what it is. Let's try a little exercise.

Step 1
Create a list of all the things that you have been avoiding because you believe that you "can't" do it. This could be submitting an article to a popular journal or becoming a part of your local writers' group. It could be that you finally sign up for that class you have been avoiding.

Step 2
Now, spend some time imagining yourself doing those things. Picture yourself sending the email to the editor or signing up to speak at an event for your chosen profession. Notice the relief you feel when you take the next step. You may find yourself wondering why you took so long to get things started.

Step 3
Then, I want you to picture yourself doing the things that you are afraid of all the time. Are you able to see the type of person you would be, always putting yourself out there without receiving

feedback, without going on the defensive, or going after your dreams without any restraint?

This is a pretty fun exercise until you do it. When these concepts are applied to our lives, things become very scary. So, what are you supposed to do? Start out small. Pick one thing that you have been avoiding and do it.

Mark Twain also said, "Eat a live frog first thing in the morning, and nothing worse will happen to you the rest of the day." Your job is to figure out what your frog is. This is your absolute worst-case scenario. Then I want you to swallow the frog.

What is it that will happen once your fears are realized? It is probably not going to be as bad as you have it in your head. Go ahead and do it. I'll wait. This will give you the chance to move on.

Did you ever play the game Red Rover as a child? You can probably hear those children screaming, "Red Rover, Red Rover, let Jane come over." You stood there, shaking, as Jane came running towards you. What did you choose to do? The only thing you thought you could do is to let go of your partner's hand. You quit. You didn't even try. And you likely felt regret after you did that.

Well, I'm giving you another chance to grab hold and not let go. The only difference is there is no threat of bodily harm. Grab up what you are afraid of and never let go. The worst thing that could happen is that you fail. You will write up something that is sub-par, or people won't understand your art. A critic may saunter along and tell you that he loathes your work. You will feel hurt.

The world will not end if you fail. It's something that everybody encounters as they work their way to success. So please, quit trying to accomplish things without fail. It's not going to work out for you. So, if you are serious about taking hold of your life, you need to learn how to fail.

Anything you do is going to take some practice. As said by Winston Churchill, "Success is stumbling from failure to failure with no loss of enthusiasm." What is it that is holding you back? It can't possibly be a failure.

Overcoming Failure
The one who failed many times are the ones that are highly successful. We tend to only know about their successes but not the struggles they went through to get to the success they currently have. We just compare ourselves to what they have achieved because we are not exposed to their mistakes and failures. This will only make it hard for us to accept the mistakes and problems that

we will encounter. We are second guessing ourselves and question our skills. We don't realize that adversity is necessary to succeed.

This thinking is the reason why the world is so scared to fail. Even at a very young age, we are told that it is terrible to be wrong and make mistakes. Even our mind will use painful memories of what has happened in the past to cause negative emotions such as anxiety and fear to keep us from making similar errors today.

J.K. Rowling, an award-winning author, embraced her failures: "It is impossible to live without failing at something unless you live so cautiously that you might as well not have lived at all – in which case, you fail by default."

Diana Nyad, a swimmer, tried five times to swim from Cuba to Florida. Alfred Nobel ended up blowing up his lab, as well as his broth, in his eventually successful attempt to create dynamite, and then ended up funding the Nobel Prize. On a recent Google Hangout with National Geographic, a group of adventurers and scientist talked about all their failures. In every single case, no matter how wrong, frustrating, or depressing the events were, their failures taught them a lesson and allowed them to be able to move forward even if they had to take a different path. Being human means that we are going to fail often.

Self-Discipline

Most scientists are wrong most of the time, and almost all athletes will end up failing most of the time when they attempt a basket, goal, or a hit. The failure rate and the heartbreak that comes along with it is all part of our everyday life. Failures and setbacks are an inevitable part of life, nobody is perfect, and we all have our own hard times. Why is it that we end up taking failure so hard? Because, we often forget that success is only achieved through trying things repeatedly and trying will usually end in failure.

One could even argue that our ability to handle failure in creative ways is what has enabled the first humans to be able to navigate around and out of Africa hundreds of thousands of years ago. Think about the number of times that small groups of our human ancestors tried to come up with functional stone tools, wooden spears, or communicate complex topics to each other, and then ended up failing. It took our ancestors almost a million years to figure out how they could control fire, to hunt big animals, and then nearly three-quarters of a million more to find out that they could paint out their lives on the walls of caves. If you look at human history, you will see more failures than success, and this is an excellent thing.

The primary way to reach success is to achieve resilience when faced with failure and persevering when you are faced with adversity, and this has been a part of our evolution. Hannah Block wrote this for National Geographic, "...without the sting of failure to spur us to reassess and rethink, progress would be impossible."

Active imagination, hope, and dreams, despite facing severe challenges, are just a part of the reason why we, as humans, have done so well. When you fail at something, it shows you your limitations, and it will force you to reevaluate or rethink how you did things. Then, you will learn how to do those things better. It will add a roadblock, make you use your brain, and ups the ante. You then must cooperate and get a little creative with your world. This is the type of thing that humans do best. Unfortunately, our society tends to view failing as a flaw, or a failure of character, and that it is a problem that must be avoided.

Let's take a moment and think about science. The most common result of any experiment is failure. The most successful scientific discoveries are created by refuting the hypothesis, by showing that they were wrong and that their first attempts failed. It's how they analyze the failures' details and reconstitute their approach that will make them succeed more. Remember how the internet, antibiotics, or electric lights were developed. Every great success had antecedents that were rife with failures. How can we then train ourselves to use these challenges to our advantage? To turn your negative experiences into positive, follow the steps below.

Accept That Failure Is Going to Happen.
When we are going through something fierce, the most frustrating thing that we can be told is to "stay positive." Everybody has already abused, misconstrued, and misused the idea of positive thinking.

Smiling and being happy through all the things that happened have very little to do with all the things we hear. If somebody says that, they are either crazy or lying. Positive thinking is used to help us evolve, learn, and grow from the things that we experience.

This does not mean that you must try to fail. All of this says that when you face a setback, you must understand that it is not the end. This is just a step on the path where you're supposed to be. When you do have to go through difficulties, it is okay for you to feel down on yourself. It is perfectly reasonable to get disappointed and upset. Your goal should be to not stay feeling down.

Release Your Frustrations.
After you have given yourself and you have cleared your mind, you will then be able to accept the things that happened. That first emotional rush you experience will eventually dissipate, and then you

will be able to slowly return your focus back to what you need to face.

Be Extremely Honest.
Take a few moments to reflect on what had happened and honestly tell yourself the reason why that situation occurred. Most people will do anything to avoid confronting their self with their own mistakes.

However, we will not learn anything if we don't take the time to do this. We may fail insanely if we don't learn from our mistakes. Albert Einstein famously explained that doing the same thing repeatedly and expecting a different result can be defined as insanity. If we can't learn from the failures and mistakes that we go through, then we will be doomed to continue repeating these mistakes.

Fail Forward.
Failing forward means that you have learned from your mistakes and adjusted it, so you succeed. Every change made, every person met, and every piece of data that you obtained is what is going to come together and give you the chance to make a different outcome.

Self-Discipline

There is no way to stop obstacles from happening, but you can learn how to handle them. They could end up blocking your vision momentarily, but if you persevere, you will find opportunities that have always been there for you that you just couldn't see. As you become more efficient with your process, you will be able to enable yourself to see that positive side of things in the hardest situations.

Not every failure will turn into success, and many are insurmountable, but that's not the point. It's our ability as humans to work our way towards goals, to hope, and to imagine the impossible that plays a vital role in the reason why we are still on this planet. The reason for human innovation is that we have hope, act on said hope, and can hold onto hope even when we are faced with a setback. So, when you end up failing, remember that you are in good company. Do what is human and get back up and try again.

Believe that you can accomplish this thing and that you are able to achieve your wildest dreams no matter what they are. If you feel stuck, find your frog and swallow it. If you end up failing, try it again. The critical thing to remember is that "can't" doesn't exist.

Chapter 5:
Developing Good Habit Fundamentals

Habits can shape our lives more than we even realize. Habits are incredibly strong. Our brains will cling to them and exclude all other things even common sense. Around 40 percent of everything we do every day is not decisions but habits we have formed.

Habits are important, and they get stronger with time and soon become second nature. You need to be sure you have the right kind of practices. Habits get their power from creating neurological cravings. When a behavior is performed, the body receives rewarded because the brain releases a pleasure chemical. Habits work on a loop:

- Trigger/cue: This could be a feeling, a person, specific time, or location

- Routine: This could be biting your nails, eating chocolate, smoking, or watching television

- Reward: Pleasure chemicals are released by the brain because of this routine.

This is a self-reinforcing mechanism that will become automatic with time. Once a habit is formed, the brain will stop participating in making decisions. Knowing how habits work on the loop will make it easier to gain control over them. When you can break down a habit into all its components, it makes it easier to change the logic of this loop. Habits get encoded into the structure of our brain and save us effort since we don't have to relearn all the things we do daily.

The Right Habits

Because our actions have become automatic, it gives us energy that we can use to focus on other tasks. This could be a good thing. If you begin to develop bad habits, you will need to interrupt it and make a new one. If you don't fight the bad habits consciously and replace them with new ones, this pattern you have created will happen automatically over, and over each time the habit gets triggered.

Your brain doesn't know the difference between good and bad habits. You must consciously decide that. You need to figure out what routines or actions you want to have and use the loop to help you. The only way to make positive changes is to turn your desired actions into habits. There is good news. Habits are not destiny. Habits can be replaced, changed or ignored. It isn't easy since habits won't ever really go away. They are only replaced by new ones.

Golden Rule

As stated above, habits won't disappear. You can't completely get rid of a bad one, you can only change it. Here is the way the Golden Rule works:

- Use the exact same trigger.

- Change up the routine.

- Give the exact same reward.

The Importance of Good Habits

- About half of the things you do daily are habits.

- Habits have power since they create neurological cravings.

- Habits work on a loop.

- Once a habit is created, the brain no longer participates in making decisions.

- Automatic actions give you the energy to be used doing other things.

- You absolutely must control your habits. Brains don't have the ability to know the difference between good and bad ones.

- Use the Golden Rule to make the correct changes.

Sleep

What you do during the day and right before you go to bed can impact your sleep. These can cause sleeplessness or promote healthy sleep. Daily routines such as what you drink and eat, how you spend your evenings, how your regular schedule plays out, and the medicines you must take can impact your sleep quality. Even a slight adjustment can mean the difference between having a sound sleep and restless nights. Writing in a sleep diary for two weeks can help you begin to understand how your routines are affecting your rest.

Sleep hygiene is healthy sleep habits that will improve your ability to go to sleep and remain asleep. These habits are the backbone of cognitive behavioral therapy. This is the most effective treatment for people who have chronic insomnia. Cognitive behavioral therapy helps address the behaviors and thoughts that keep us from sleeping. It also gives you techniques to help reduce stress, relax, and schedule a sleep routine. If you have problems sleeping and need improving your sleep, try to follow these healthy habits. Speak with your physician if your problems persist.

Quick Tips

You can use the tips to create some healthy sleep habits:

- Keep a constant schedule. At the same time each day including weekends and on vacations, you need to get up.

- Have a bedtime that gets you in bed early enough that you will get no less than seven hours of sleep.

- Never go to bed if you aren't sleepy.

- If after 20 minutes, you haven't fallen asleep, get up.

- Create a bedtime routine that is relaxing.

- Use the bed for only sex and sleep.

- Your bedroom needs to be relaxing and quiet. Keep the room at a cool but comfortable temperature.

- Limit the amount of time you are exposed to bright light during the evenings.

- Turn off all electronic devices 30 minutes before going to bed.

- Never eat large meals before bedtime. If you feel hungry, try eating a light snack that is healthy.

- Eat a healthy diet and get regular exercise.

- Don't drink caffeine during the late afternoon or evenings.

- Don't drink alcohol before going to bed.

- Don't drink a lot of fluids before you go to bed.

Diet

To maintain a healthy lifestyle, you need to create healthy eating habits and stick with them. Exercise is just 50 percent of the health equation. The other half is nutrition. If you don't have healthy eating habits, you aren't going to be able to have good fitness and health. What you eat does play a factoring role in your health and in this modern day of rushed schedules and convenience, it is effortless to eat things that aren't healthy. Here are some things to think about that will keep you on track.

Get Educated

You need to know what foods are healthy and the ones that aren't. You could talk to your doctor or a dietician to help you get started. Do some research on the web or find some books about nutrition. Most foods you get from fast food restaurants, or convenience stores are loaded with sugar, salt, and many other unhealthy ingredients. These ingredients are usually hidden, so you need to know how to read a food label.

Know what ingredients you need to stay away from. The main ingredients are always listed first. Look at and compare fat content because most foods that are promoted as low fat are most of the time very high in fat. Knowing what is in most foods will help you find the unhealthy one you might otherwise eat.

Substitute Ingredients and Foods

Back in the day, when someone wanted to eat healthily, it meant eating bland foods that had absolutely no taste. Remember when veggie burgers tasted like cardboard? Those days are behind us as technology has dramatically improved. Most of the low-fat versions of foods such as frozen yogurt and cheese taste as good as the full-fat versions.

You can also cook great tasting food by substituting some simple ingredients. Begin using olive oil instead of butter to fry. Lessen the amount of salt by adding spices. Find leaner cuts of meat and trim off any visible fat before you cook it. You could also cut back on eating red meat and eat more poultry and fish. Find some recipes that use chicken and fish. You will be amazed that you don't even miss red meat.

The most significant area to work on is your snacks. Don't reach for the potato chips and chocolate bars. Instead, reach for fruit or nuts. During hot summer days, freeze some grapes for a healthy, midday cooling snack.

Keep Your Goals in Mind
To help you stick with your healthy habits after you have created them, you need to keep your goals in mind. If your goal is maintaining those abs that you have worked hard to get, each time you look in the mirror, check their condition to make sure you continue to eat right.

You might also like to ski during the winter months. If you want to perform well on the slopes, keep this goal in mind to keep you fit all year long. Find other related activities that you would like to do well and relate them back to nutrition. When you follow these things in mind, you will be able to stay away from bad foods. You don't want to blame a bad performance on a bad diet.

Stay Around People Who Eat Healthily

You need to have people around you that will help you keep your goals. It is hard to eat right when everyone around you is eating unhealthily. Be sure you spend time with people who eat healthy, too. This will inspire you to keep eating healthy. You are using teamwork to help you get to your goal of eating healthy.

There isn't a magic potion on how to create healthy eating habits and making them stick. Having good health is a life-long commitment, and the easiest way to achieve it is by all the little goals you have reached when you eat a healthy meal and complete another exercise routine. If you can follow these tips, you will eventually have optimum health.

Exercise

The biggest problem with trying to create a habit of exercising is that you try to do it three or four times every week and this just makes it too hard. The reason behind this is the more constant an action is, there is a more likelihood of it becoming a habit.

Exercising daily will more than likely result in a habit. It will become automatic and more natural instead of always struggling with it. You can implement this into your daily life, too. You can alternate different exercises each day like strength training, biking, swimming or running. You might have a goal of competing in a marathon. The only way of doing this is to make running a daily habit. If you are dedicated to making this a habit, here are some tips that will help you make exercise a daily practice:

Pick a specific time. Figure out a time that you will stick with whether it be during the evening, lunchtime or mornings. You must stick with this time. If you don't choose a specific time, you might put it off until the next day or when you have more energy or time. Soon, this will never be a habit at all.

Send reminders to yourself. Many apps will send you reminders either by text or email. This way, you won't ever forget. When you get the reminder, do it right then. Don't delay.

Begin small. This is the most useful of the suggestions. When you begin exercising, you will have massive amounts of energy, ambition, and enthusiasm. You will think you can do more than you can. Doing too much at first could lead to burnout, and this will lead to stopping your habit. When you just begin making exercise a daily habit, your body isn't going to be used to dealing with the stress you are putting on it. The main thing is to only do about 20 minutes when you begin. Take is easy. Don't do anything hard. Even doing 10 to 15 minutes is better than nothing. The key is getting out there. Slowly get your body used to exercising daily and create that habit.

Progress later. When your body is finally used to exercising daily, you can slowly begin to increase the intensity and amount of your exercises. Wait about two weeks before starting an increase. This is the minimum that your body needs to get adjusted. When it begins to feel too easy, this is the time to increase the length of your routines to 30 or 40 minutes. You will eventually be about to do it for an hour. When you can work out for an hour, and it feels relatively easy, begin increasing the intensity, like running harder or faster. Try not to increase both strength and distance at the same time.

Make it fun. If you connect a habit with pain, you won't do it. If it is fun, you will want to do it. When you are beginning an exercise routine, the more fun it is, the more you will be willing to do it. If you are running, go slow at first; enjoy the scenery, fresh air, beautiful skies, the solitude, the sun rises or sets, and contemplation. Make it something you enjoy doing. Listening to music helps, too.

Lay out the gear. If your new habit doesn't create any friction and doesn't have any obstacles, it will be more of a success. If you are getting up early to run, you don't want to have to gather up all your gear when you are still half asleep. You may just crawl back into bed. If you lay out your clothing, shoes, mp3 player, and watch, you will be ready to head out the door in no time at all without having to face obstacles.

Self-Discipline

Get out the door. Plan to get your shoes on and get out the door. Don't worry about how long the run is going to be or how hard it might be. Just get out the door and get it started. Once you are out the door, the rest is a piece of cake.

Mix it up. When you mix things up, you will have a variety of activities to do. This makes things more interesting. It is just as important that with each exercise, you are training different muscles, especially if you are swimming. Some muscles are being constantly used, but they get used differently with different stresses being put on them. What this means is that you aren't pounding the same muscles each day. This gives them the time to recover. If you don't let them heal, you will break your muscles down with time.

Have a day of rest. Recovery is significant. Therefore, you should let your body rest. If you are going slow and just doing 20 minutes, you are going to be fine without having rest days. It is still good to have a day of rest. A day where you aren't doing the exercises, you do the other days. You don't ever want to skip a day entirely since you won't be consistent with the habit. Try doing a day of strength training. You won't be using the same muscles as you are the other six days. If your muscles need more rest, you could just try to do a day of walking or try meditation. The main point is to do something each day that will keep your habit going.

Stephen Patterson

Never skip a day. It is easy to train for five days then tell yourself you've been good, and you deserve a down day. This will make forming this habit harder. Being constant is the key. Try not to skip a day. If you do, you don't have to beat yourself up about it. Never judge. Never feel bad. Everybody slips up every now and then. Forming habits is a skill that takes practice. Just start it back the next day and find the obstacle that caused you to skip a day. Be prepared for it this time.

Chapter 6:
Vocabulary for Success

Many people will use phrases like: "I wish I could," "I don't know how," "I can't," and "I won't" in their everyday talk. It is fine to use these words if the situation demands it. People who use these self-limiting lingos regularly are subconsciously tunneling themselves into a life of self-doubt, powerlessness, and limitations. In other words, somebody that uses phrases like: "This is going to be mine," "I am," and "I can" will attract abundance, success, and achievement just because this type of language puts them into the right frame of mind to succeed.

When you constantly use phrases like the above, you will end up feeling miserable, victimized, and anguished even if you did your best in these situations.

When you work through your problems by thinking you can, you achieved great results even if you didn't have the best solution when you began. You believed you could and found a way to work through the problems.

What category do you fall under? Do you use self-doubting and negative lingo daily? How do you begin using language that empowers such as "I will," "I can," "I will get it finished?" You just need to replace that negative lingo with the empowering lingo.

While working on your language, remember that language can affect a person's self-confidence instead of being the cause. Build your self-confidence and self-belief at the same time. You might be in a meeting and immediately felt the vibe in the room change just because someone said something.

Words are powerful. Even one word can change how others see you, set your boundaries, put you out, and win you over. With this type of power, it is best to understand the psychology and science of words. Here are the top ten phrases and words that will motivate us:

If: Describes A Positive Hypothetical; Improves Performance

Here is a universal truth. Nobody likes to be wrong, especially if you are in front of other people. When you face many "I don't know" during a tough challenge or brainstorming session, the small word "if" could alleviate the pressure of being wrong and open a path to critical thinking. Here is a specific sentence that you should use a lot: "What would you say if you did know?"

By using the little word "if," it lets others you are talking to think hypothetically. This takes all the pressure away that prevents them from answering. When you can describe a hypothetical outcome positively, it will increase their expectation for success and improves their performance. The key is the hypothetical element and it needs to be triggered by "if".

Could: Use This in Place of Should to Get Creative

Magic also happens when you use the word "could" especially if you substitute it for the word "should." These two words sound very similar, but research shows us that "should" will narrow a person's field of vision and will limit potential answers. The word "could" will open a person's mind to new possibilities.

When talking about ethical dilemmas, shifting your mindset from "What should I do?" to "What could I do?" will generate a moral insight. This is defined as realizing that competing values aren't incompatible. You can change to a new train of thought just by choosing a different word.

Yes: Three Yeses Can Close A Deal

Yes, is another small magic word. It is very interesting to see how one yes can lead to another. One study looked at the possibility that getting someone to say yes while conversing would affect the entire outcome of the conversation. First, a salesperson did business as usual and was able to close about 18 percent of the sales. They were then instructed to get the customers to say yes three times early in the conversation. Suddenly, they were closing on 32 percent of the sales. Tiny yeses can be any type of affirmative such as responding to a question such as "You are here for the four o'clock appointment, right?"

Together: Will Make Teams Work Smarter and Harder
The word together is about interconnectivity, belonging, and relatedness. This is powerful things for our brains because belonging is very elemental to our hierarchy of needs. It isn't surprising that using the word "together" can help people become more efficient.

Participant worked on hard puzzles by themselves. One group was told they would work together and would receive tips from other members. The group who heard "together" had astounding results. These people:

- Had better recall on what they saw.

- Worked almost 50 percent longer.

- Said the puzzle was more interesting.

- Solved problems correctly.

- Said they weren't as tired by the task.

The word together will motivate you to feel like you are part of something larger than yourself. Words like "we" and "let's" can build a sense of togetherness and connection.

Thank You: Makes People Likely to Seek Out Relationships
Gratitude not only makes our lives happier, but it can also help you further your career and relationships. Research shows that when you thank someone for their help, it makes them want to seek out an ongoing relationship with you.

One study of students that provided advice to young students showed that only a few were thanked for their help. The ones who were thanked provided their contact details when asked for it like their email address or phone number. The students who said "thank you" were also said to have warmer personalities. When you say, "thank you", it shows others that you are a person they can have a quality relationship with. There are five elements to an effective thank you:

- Compliment the benefactor's attributes
- Recognize the benefactor's costs
- Be timely
- Recognize the benefactor's intent
- Articulate the benefits

Choose To: Use Instead Of "Have To"
Completing an exercise that is called "have to" to "choose to" can change your life in a huge way.

Step One: What happens in your life that you don't think is playful? Write out on a piece of paper all the things that you must do. List all activities that you don't like but do because you think you don't have a choice.

Step Two: After you have finished your list, clearly define all the things you do just because you choose to, not because you must. Insert words like "I choose to..." in front of everything you have listed.

Step Three: After you have acknowledged that you have chosen to do a certain activity, find out the intention behind your choice by completing this statement, "I choose to... because I want ..."

And: This Is the Best Way to Put A Contrary Opinion

If you need to disagree with somebody, express your opinion as an "and." It isn't necessary for another person to be wrong and for you to be right. When you are surprised to hear what the other person has said, don't interrupt with "That isn't right!" You only must add your perspective. Say this instead: "You are saying we need to keep room in the budget for the event, and I am worried about money for the employees to be trained. Do we have any options?" Here are some other phrases that will help you be heard:

- "I came to this conclusion because..."

- "Do you see any flaws with my reasoning?"

- "I would love to hear your reactions to what I said."

- "Here is what I am thinking."

- "Do you see the situation differently?"

- "My perspective is based on the following assumptions..."

Because: This Word Can Make You Feel Rational and Objective

One of the two very important words in blogging is also a top one for motivating people: Because. Ellen Langer, a social psychologist, tested this word by asking people to get in front of them in line at a copy place. She used three different variations:

- "Excuse me, I have five pages. May I use the copy machine?"

- "Excuse me, I have five pages. May I use the copy machine because I am in a hurry?"

- "Excuse me, I have five pages. May I use the copy machine because I have to make some copies?"

Around 60 percent of the people she asked allow her in front of them when she used the first technique. When she added the 'because', one rated at 93 percent and the other at 94 percent. When you would like people to act, you need to give them a reason. When you use cause and effect reasoning, it works because it makes your request sound rational and objective instead of subjective and biased. Here is a list of cause and effect phrases:

- Thus

- Therefore

Self-Discipline

- Since
- For this reason
- Due to
- Consequently
- Caused by
- As a result
- Accordingly

You could take this a step further with what is called the Advanced Because Technique. The idea behind this is to get you to say because to yourself. Instead of giving another person thousands of reasons to try something, ask them "Why?" Once you can do that, they will figure out their own because. It is now their reasons, and no longer your problem.

Other's Names: We Like Things That Are Connected to Us

Virginia has 30 percent more people that are named Virginia than any other state. Louisiana has 37 percent more people named Louis than any other state. Georgia has 88 percent Georgia's than any other state.

This is called the Name-Letter Effect. This is a weird phenomenon that shows most people possess associations about themselves and prefer things that connect to that self. A person's name is the most important and sweetest sound in any language. There is evidence that certain brain patterns can happen when we hear our names as opposed to hearing other people's names.

Willing: This Could Turn A "No" Into A "Yes"

While answering hundreds of calls between potential clients and mediators, Elizabeth Stoke discovered a magic word that changed minds: "Willing." Most callers were ready to reject mediation because they thought the other party was a person who wouldn't mediate.

When the mediator asked a person if they were "willing" to mediate, even the most resistant caller agreed to try their service. "Willing" was more effective than any other phrase like "you might be interested in mediation." "Willing" was the only word that changed a no to a yes. This works because if one party is a person who won't mediate, then the person calling will be. Here is a list of words you need to stop using immediately:

- Fast

- Just

Self-Discipline

- Easy
- Can't
- Must
- Need
- Ugly
- Not enough
- Stupid
- Never
- Busy

More importantly these negative words are the true heavy hitters that should not be used:

Only. This one works with the word "just," too. You might have caught yourself using the word only such as "I only walked five miles today." "I'm emailing you just to tell you...", "I just started yoga today." It is time to stop doing that. Stay away from thinking about any day as a test to your character. It doesn't matter if you ran three blocks or three miles. Today isn't about you personally. Take each day as a day to progress a little farther. People that approach goals and challenges with a mindset of growing instead of as a test won't see any setbacks as failures but opportunities to learn better habits and develop better skills. If you don't run as far as you wanted, it is fine. Tomorrow is another day, and you will do it then.

Fat: This word works along with "ugly." Women are very guilty of telling themselves they are ugly. It is human nature to self-depreciate. To be able to form more accurate and better self-images, you must get rid of all negative adjectives. Stop yourself from using self-defeating talk and make conscious choices to change. You aren't fat, you are getting healthy. You might not believe this at first, but if you can learn to use positive language, you will soon talk yourself into thinking it.

Too much. This one goes with the phrase above, too. It is easy to think we are too much wrong or not enough right. This just reinforces all the embedded presupposition factors in the brain. If you were to ask yourself, "Why aren't I enough?" your brain will immediately begin looking for answers. It acts as an internet search. You will find what you are looking for eventually. Instead of assuming you aren't good enough, think about affirmations. These will reframe the questions that lead your mind to search for answers and stay away from the endless repetition of the common affirmations. Ask yourself: "Why am I enough?" When you do this, you are setting your brain on the correct path, and you might be delightfully surprised with what your mind comes up with.

Won't. This word works along with the word can't. When you tell yourself that you can't eat a hamburger or you won't lose weight when you don't work out, this is working against you. When trying to make change happen, you must avoid negative language. You need to fill your mind with definite ideas. If you don't, you are going to confuse it with unfavorable terms. The brain will drop the won't or can't and will focus on what you would like to do. Many times, all those won't or can't statements just aren't true. Try to focus on what you will and can do. Tell yourself things such as: "I can have a cheat meal today," "There are a lot of delicious and healthy snacks that will keep me full," "I will lose weight because I am working out each day." There is only one exception to this rule, and that is your physical limitations. If you can't eat a food because of food allergies or workout due to a physical handicap or injury, your mind might remind you to protect itself. Try to keep your eyes on what you can do instead of what you can't.

Failure: When you call yourself a failure, this is the best way to make yourself fail at everything you try. You are fulfilling your own self-prophecy. You need to be the best positive coach you can be to yourself. When you do that, you take "I'm not good" and change it into "I am good, and I can do this"; or "I'm a failure" into "I have failed but also won, I will win this time, too." You also don't want to lie to yourself. You need to make room for disappointments. If you expect perfection, you are going to fail. You must forgive yourself, be patient with changing and let yourself grow.

Lucky: There are going to be days that you feel fortunate, and that is wonderful. You shouldn't use luck as a reason for why you can't do something or to discredit somebody else. You can have luck, but it must be used with hard work to accomplish things. Don't compare your life with other people's lives. While you envy somebody's legs, arms, or abs, don't ever say they are lucky. Tell yourself that they worked hard to get the body they have, and you can have the same rock-hard abs if you work hard at it, too.

Tomorrow: If you consistently put things off until another day, you are never going to get them done. One common trap is saying, "I didn't eat right today, so I'll start my diet tomorrow." This lets you keep delaying it, and it will never really start. Try to pick a realistic and concrete begin date and stick with it. You must make yourself accountable. If you aren't going to do it tomorrow, when are you doing to do it? You also need to have a reason behind the diet to stay motivated. You need to know "why" and not just "how." It doesn't matter if you are trying to lower your blood pressure, stop

Self-Discipline

smoking, and the risk of diabetes. You are setting an excellent example for your children. You might want to get fit so you can look great in your swimsuit next summer, choose a reason and remind yourself daily.

When you are working with others, be careful of using the above words. Watch out when you use them. Watch out when you hear them. These could really get you in trouble.

Chapter 7:
Strategies for Self-Discipline

We aren't born having self-discipline. It is something we develop with time. It is much like strengthening our muscles. To start creating self-discipline, you need certain factors to happen. Some of these things will come from inside you and others will come from external sources. Let's explore some of these factors.

You Need A Why

To develop self-discipline, you need to have a desire to reach a goal. Without this desire, there isn't much hope in having self-discipline.

Self-discipline requires fuel, and this comes from either motivation or inspiration. You need one of the two to give ammunition to your self-discipline. If not, you might struggle to remain focused over long time periods. This basically boils down to having enough reasons to undertake every task you commit to doing. You need to ask yourself these questions:

- What exactly is it that I want?

- Why do I desire this?

- What do I need to do specifically to get this done?

- The better the reasons you can identify, the more fuel you must drive forward your self-discipline.

Unmoving Accountability and Commitment

Reasons aren't enough. You need the commitment to do whatever is required to get to your goal. It isn't ever easy. Long-term commitment does take discipline, and typically, this isn't something that many people are good at. Most people just lack some accountability. Long-term commitments require we hold ourselves accountable or have somebody else hold us accountable. Both methods will work. If they can work together, this is when you will get the best results.

Requires Rewards and Penalties

Levels of motivation can come and go as we move forward toward our goals. There will be a time when we feel very motivated and others we might struggle to get through certain activities or tasks during out day.

To stop falling into these cycles, it would be helpful to implement some rewards and penalties. Awards and punishments could be used to direct your behavior through the day.

You can give yourself a reward for making certain choices of acting a certain way. You could also penalize yourself for engaging in harmful behaviors or making bad decisions. These rewards and penalties add another element to your internal desires that keep the fire of self-discipline burning bright during your day.

Personal Standards

If there is any lack of self-discipline in any parts of your life, it is because you don't hold yourself accountable for keeping certain standards. These standards you keep will keep you on target while you are working toward your goal. These are unspoken rules that will guide your actions, behavior, decisions, and choices through your day. Keep that in mind while we outline some standards you should uphold while pursuing your goals. Ask yourself these questions:

- If I get off track, how can I correct things?

- Are there any choices and behaviors I will not tolerate?

Self-Discipline

- Are there any choices and behaviors that I will accept?

- What standards am I going to uphold?

This basically comes down to making an agreement with yourself. Knowing what you will or won't accept are the basics for self-discipline. You will then have to keep yourself accountable for following through on these agreements. You must regulate and correct your behavior when you get off track. This is what self-discipline is about. There is one more point we still need to talk about. That is the environment.

Competitive Environment
The last layer requires you to make a competitive environment that will drive you toward your goal. This isn't saying you are competing with other people. You can place yourself into a frame of mind where you try to outperform and outwork others. This is one way to discipline yourself. There is one other way to do this, too. You need to compete against your best self. You need to measure your current results against your past performance and can be useful when helping you stay disciplined, motivated, and focused. It might just be the main ingredient that fuels your self-discipline when things don't go your way.

Chapter 8:
Controlling Your Environment

Many people think that intentions are followed by habits. Truthfully, the primary purpose of the brain is to look for patterns and use it as shortcuts so it can process all the information, we receive every day. We rely on environmental triggers more than we think we do. Researchers have found that students who transferred to a new school changed their habits. It is observed that if they were not exposed to normal cues, it is much easier for them to break the habit.

The example above proves the research conducted with regards to the stimulus control theory. The effect of the stimulus on behavior can be described by the example. These techniques can even be used to help insomnia patients. People who have problems fallings asleep were told to just lie down on their bed if they were tired. If they still can't fall asleep, they can go and try in a different room.

This advice may be strange, but eventually, researchers saw that by connecting bed with "time to sleep" and not any other activities

Self-Discipline

like watching television or reading, subjects were able to fall asleep because this process is repeated. Since the trigger has been created, it becomes automatic to fall asleep when they head to bed. Maybe we are like Pavlov's dog after all. Finding out how our behavior can be impacted by just little cues can somehow be scary. Eating with a large spoon will make you eat more. Chewing on a big plate will make you eat more. You won't eat as much chocolate if you move it away from your desk.

- Good behavior can be encouraged by these triggers.

Change your behavior using your environment. Just like how muscles can be worn out, discipline also does as well. You can use environmental changes to help you do hard tasks. Here are some methods to help you develop this:

Task Association

To be able to write well, you must be able to read well. When you write on the internet, this can become a problem since you can quickly turn on your next inspiration.

One method that you can use is to set up specific devices to do specific activities. Your office needs to be designated to only a workspace. Don't fill the room or space with fun things to do. You can also choose a location outside your home. These are sometimes more effective. You can go to a library or a coffee shop if you have some writings to do which will become associated with the time to write.

Increase or Reduce Friction

Making specific tasks harder or easier to can be affected by the environment. If your goals cannot guide you to make behaviors easier, it can be harmful. Instead of focusing on doing an individual behavior, it is much better to focus on making the action easier instead. You need to get rid of times when you just want to give up. You can make these moments more intense if you're going to prevent yourself from making a bad habit.

Habits are a way to simplify movements that are needed to get a particular result. Increasing friction is an excellent way to influence your behavior. Since willpower is fragile, focus your energies on making hard habits harder to do. If you want to reduce friction, the best example is the "hit the ground running" with your most healthy habit.

If you have a hard time getting out the door every morning, put your gym clothes in your bag and place it by the door. Put your purse and jacket on the counter next to the door. When you have high willpower, get rid of any excuse. Don't force habits. Take some effort and make good habits easier to do and bad habits harder to engage with.

Use Contextual Cues

It is easier to build a constant habit when you create it off an existing one. To simplify, one task will get more natural if it is either followed or preceded by another job you enjoy. Since the second task happens at every day at the same time, it is easy to build on top of it since there is a trigger you can rely on each day. Try to schedule tasks during constant times of your schedule like after or during lunch, when you wake up, as soon as you get home.

Have Routines

Things don't always happen in one night. Performing the same habit repeatedly can result in success. Research has found that having too many choices is the long-term goal's enemy. Having a lot of options makes consistent behavior harder to do. You need to practice making routines out of the essential aspects of your life to maintain consistency. You can be aggressive in other parts of your life.

A good example is the average spending versus saving don't rely on willpower alone to save money. Take this decision away by having withdrawals taken out of our paycheck into a savings account. This will let you worry less about spending since the banking system has taken care of this for you by getting rid of the money before you have a chance to see it. This small change can have an impact since it will compound if you do it right. Find the areas in your life that you think are mundane, and then make a routine out of these aspects when you can. Try to make fewer decisions.

Chapter 9: Develop Drive

It is normal to need a boost after you have worked all day. Motivators such as praise and money will only get you so far. They might kickstart your journey, but they won't get you to the finish line. You are going to need a strong inner drive when obstacles get in your way. Here are some ways to strengthen your internal drive:

Journal

This one might take some work to become a habit, but it will be totally worth it. Journaling won't just document your journey; it is a way for you to get rid of all your feelings and thoughts so you can focus on what matters. Write down your goals, list things you are grateful for, record what you did during the week. Had a hard day at work? Write it down. Did something happen to inspire you? Write it down. After you have written in a journal for a while, you will realize you have a clearer head. You can even go back through to reminisce later.

Get Involved in The Community

It might be professional or personal but being a part of your community is a wonderful way to get your inner drive going. A group of people who are all working for a common goal will keep you motivated when you slip up. A community that is supportive makes you excited to go to work. Networking events, groups, co-working spaces, or online forums can be a great help when you need some motivation. If you want to work on the personal end of your drive, community centers, mentors, and local meetups are great places to begin.

Educate Other People

When you take the time to help educate people, it has a lot of personal benefits. You might not realize how much you know until you teach it to somebody else. This can boost your confidence. When educating others, it might be one person or a whole workshop; you are saying that you are successful and a reliable source of wisdom.

People will seek you out if they have a question about your expertise. That should give you enough motivation to hone your skills and work toward your goals. It is great to realize you have gone far enough to be able to teach others how to succeed the way you have. You must continually push yourself a bit harder to maintain this status.

Visualize Success

What is it going to look like when you finally reach your goals? Will you be taking the vacation of your dreams? You must look past the material rewards and focus on social and personal. Is it going to give you more family time every week? Will you be the main speaker at next year's conference?

Many people who can envision success can motivate them to push them toward their goals. Other people can make their conceptions concrete by creating a vision board. You can make this with a corkboard, some notebook paper or on Pinterest. Try to find pictures that show your idea of success. It might be images of a beach or photos of the family. If you can keep your vision board where you can see it, you will be reminded of why you must keep pushing forward, even when things get hard.

Practice Optimism

To quote Henry Ford: "Whether you think you can, or you think you can't, you're right." You might have seen this quote many times, and it still holds true. Your attitude is your primary ability to reach your goals. You can maintain a positive manner by using optimism during the day. Don't think you are bad at something; just tell yourself you are working on it. Don't focus on how much you hate doing something; look forward to things that excite you.

Stephen Patterson

Optimism isn't going to lead to success. You are still going to have to find resources and put in some effort. It will help you get there. When you feel like you are losing steam, a strong inner drive keeps you moving forward.

Chapter 10:
Directing Your Attention

A wise man gave his protégé this riddle to solve: "You possess a potent tool – one that is always with you. You could use this tool any time to make decisions more efficiently, to make interactions with others more rewarding, and to find more joy in life. What is this amazing tool?"

This man studied a lot for years but couldn't solve this riddle. He was sitting on a bus one day and saw a couple in the seat next to him. The woman was talking to the man she was sitting with, the man wasn't listening as he was reading the newspaper. The girl seated in front of him was listening to her iPod while sending text messages. This man almost solved this riddle when he heard a noise and looked outside. He then realized he should have gotten off the bus two stops earlier. He had not been paying attention.

Attention and the ability to focus on it is the most powerful skill that we own. Many of us go through life without paying any attention to notice. That can cost us a lot. We could lose the ability to participate now. We may think we save time when we plan our meals while our partner talks about their day. What we are doing is robbing our partners and ourselves of the opportunity to connect deeper and be intimate.

Paying attention to just one thing at a time can give us many rewards including more joy out of life, more satisfying personal interactions, and decreased anxiety. Paying attention does take some practice, but it is a needed skill and one that is worth honing.

Attention Deficit

Think about attention as a flashlight. When you use it in the best way, we can light up a single object and be able to see it clearly. Focusing our attention this way is a lot easier said than done.

The hard part is trying to keep the flashlight focused on just one thing at a time through circumstance and hardwiring. Our brains are multifaceted and complex. They can engage in more than one thing at a time. In this high demand, fast-paced world, it usually comes with undesirable consequences and hidden costs.

One thing we always attempt involves focusing our attention on an internal and external stimulant at the same time. We might be trying to listen to our best friend tell about her breakup while going through the pantry in your mind trying to figure out what you are going to make for supper.

This usually doesn't work too well. When our attention gets split like this, we miss a lot of things that come at us. The more substantial cost might manifest itself in the form of emotional stress. Self-focused attention creates an endless loop where we think about what we are thinking about. This cycle tends to bring on worry and anxiety.

People that suffer from social anxiety like the fear of speaking in public focus on their own internal negative assumptions about certain situations instead of the world around us. This can lead to stress that distorts our view of our public interaction and performance. This, in turn, creates even more anxiety.

Many psychologists and psychiatrists believe emotional distress happens when we focus on ourselves too much. When we only focus inward, we can see the beauty around us. We suffer since our attention will pull us toward either the past or future instead of letting us stay in the present. This leads to feeling distressed like anxiety, food cravings, depression, and shyness.

Training Our Focus

To develop being able to focus our attention, we must overcome some obstacles. Being preoccupied is a significant enemy of focused attention. Another one is passive entertainment. Television moving at fast paces trains our brains to lose interest in things that don't move at high rates of speed. Multitasking is another thing that is hard to stay away from. Having a multitasking mind isn't efficient. It will rob you of being fully immersed in any activity.

Realizing these obstacles would be the first step to help sharpen our attention skills. You need to know where your focus is at. You could use an alarm on your watch to help you with that. You could set it to signal every 45 minutes. When you hear the alarm, you would stop and take notice of what you are doing. If you are worried about bills, or what a coworker said earlier in the day, you aren't paying attention to what is happening right now. Here are some strategies to help you shift your attention:

- Use large muscles. Go for a job or play handball.

- Begin a non-repetitive activity like gardening or cooking.

- Pick a fast-paced activity instead of a slow one. Go skiing instead of reading a book.

Self-Discipline

Activities that focus your mind and move your body will help shift your attention. You are going to find psychological relief, be in the moment, and find joy in everything you do.

Activities that focus your mind and move your body will help shift your attention. You are going to find psychological relief, be in the moment, and find joy in everything you do.

When you invest in developing your attention skills, you will be bettering every aspect of your life. The world comes alive when you can pay attention to it. There's no better time like the present to begin. You can master your attention skill by practicing. Here are two exercises to help you with this skill:

Do Only One Thing. Multitasking is typical for many people, but would your life fall apart if you stopped trying to do everything? Just experiment and see. Take a day and focus on just doing one thing at a time. When you are watching the news, just sit and watch the news. When you are talking to your best friend on the phone, give them your undivided attention to them. When you are eating, just eat. Turn off the television, put down the magazine, and turn off the computer. You might be surprised how great experiences can be when you give them your undivided attention.

Stephen Patterson

Get Blue. Look for blue for an entire day. Actively scan for blue. From the smallest speck on a movie poster to the enormous expanse of sky. Make blue the focus of a mental treasure hunt that you will win all day.

Chapter 11: Social Motivation

Social motives can be defined as complex motive states. These get classified as social since they are learned in social groups such as families. They are also called secondary or learned motives. There are various social motives. We are going to look at the four most common reasons. These are:

Need for Achievement

This one is the most important of all. It's mainly concerned with setting goals and then achieving them. It wants to be successful in whatever it does. It wants to always avoid failing. People who have powerful achievement motives don't just want to be better than others but try to do better than they have done in the past.

People who have this high need to achieve will do better in school, their jobs, and all areas of their life. People will choose tasks that are not too easy or difficult but ones that they are confident they can accomplish with doing their best. The need to achieve can be influenced by these factors:

Trained to Be Independent as A Child
People who have the need for achievement usually come from families that have taught them to be independent since their childhood. Some are even given the freedom to do what they want to do.

Socio-Cultural Environment
This can also be a factor for having the need for achievement. In certain societies such as the Zuni Indians and the Arapesh of New Guinea, this is not a factor for them. The average American is in extreme need for achievement when compared to the average Indian.

Success from The Past
People who have a history of success in a task also have a high need for achievement when compared to people that have a history of failure.

Sex
This doesn't seem probable, but this can also influence a person's need for achievement. Women usually have lower requirements for performance when compared to men. Many women will suppress their need for achievement out of fear of success since success in the traditional text doesn't always bring social progress.

Self-Discipline

There has been a lot of work done on the need for achievement. This is related to economic growth. Societies who have a need for achievement also have a higher rate of economic growth as compared to communities who don't have a need for success.

Tests have been created to measure the need for achievement and social motives. Projective tests are what is generally used as the measurement for the need for success. One test is called the Thematic Apperception Test or TAT. Here are some characteristics of people who have a high need for achievement:

People who have a need for a result like working on challenging tasks that will get them success. They don't work on easy tasks where they aren't being tested because it isn't giving them any achievement. They also don't like functions that are extremely hard as they might fail at something.

- They like tasks where their performance gets compared to others. They love having feedback on how they are doing.

- They like working on things that are related to their career or that reflect their personal characteristics like intelligence. All this helps them to get ahead.

- When these people are successful, they will raise their expectations to a point where they can move on to a bit more difficult and challenging tasks.

- These people like to work in situations where they have control over its outcome. They aren't gamblers, though.

Power Motivation or Need for Power

The need for power is defined as the need to charm, lead, persuade, cajole, control, or influence others and to better their reputation with others. People who have a strong need for power get satisfaction from reaching their goals.

The need for power can be expressed in several ways: the degree of what the person fears about their own need for control, how mature they are, sex, and their socio-economic status. Here are some ways that people who have a need for power express themselves:

- Aggressive and impulsive actions.

- Playing competitive sports like swimming, boxing, football, hockey, etc.

- Joining an organization and then holding an office in that organization.

Self-Discipline

- With men: sexually dominating women and drinking.

- By obtaining possessions like a lot of credit cards, huge stereo equipment, guns, fancy cars, etc.

- Being around people who aren't very popular and who might be easy to control.

- Choosing careers like clergy, business owners, diplomacy, and teaching where they will be able to impact others.

- Disciplining and building their bodies. This holds very true for women who have a very strong need for power.

The concept of Machiavellianism is related to the need for power. This term was coined by psychologists to describe people that express their motivation to exploit and manipulate others in dishonest and deceptive ways.

Human Aggression

This can be defined as any behavior that is directed to a goal of injuring or harming another being who is trying to stay away from this treatment. Aggression could be indirect or direct, passive or active, verbal or physical.

There have been many theories about aggression. One popular approach to aggression is that it's instinctive in nature. Some researchers believe that aggression is the result of social and environmental factors. Aggression could have been caused by many social and environmental factors. Some of these are:

- Negative evaluation or verbal insult from other people.

- Being obedient to authority.

- Intense noise and crowding.

- Aggression is thought to be a learned behavior and is learned by many different learning principles.

Need for Affiliation
This common social motive relates to maintaining and expressing attitudes of loyalty to friends and family, winning other's affections, pleasing others, and interacting with peers.

Chapter 12: Measuring Progress

Being able to measure your progress is reasonable for many people. It isn't normal to be able to measure progress well. This can lead to misjudgments. You need to think about your progress more and make them a constant source for good.

Measuring can tell you how you are doing and the progress you have made. Checking on progress can help get you motivated. It can help you know if you have been slacking and will tell you if you need to change your course.

If you aren't thinking about the way you measure your progress, you might be measuring the wrong things or measuring it the wrong way. You could debilitate it or fall behind on a project or even miss out on opportunities. If you measure progress, you must do it right. Turn off the automatic gut and measure your progress mindfully.

Measure Your Process Goals

If you are a Type A person, you have probably overworked yourself, thinking that working more will give you more progress. Will it? Have you taken the time to measure? Just because you are stressed and overworked doesn't mean you are getting anything accomplished. You must figure out how far you are from your goal and if you are closing the gap.

You need to figure out what goals you are chasing. You need to know the difference between process and outcome goals. Outcome goals, such as wanting a promotion, are something you can strive to get. It isn't anything that you can do. Process goals are actions that can be measured. These could help you get closer to the outcome goal.

You need to measure your progress daily by moving toward your process goals. How much you work doesn't matter. What matters is the work that will take you closer to reaching your daily process goal. After that, you need to check to see if your process goals are doing what they are supposed to do and that is keeping track of your movements toward your outcome goal.

Let's say you work in sales and you need to make 30 cold calls every day. If you only send email, you can't count this as progress. If your outcome goal is to close sales, and you haven't locked any in a long time, you need to rethink your process goals. The number of calls isn't leading to sales. You need to make more progress on the quality of these calls. Make a new process goal by tweaking your sales pitch and work toward that.

Measure the Distance You Have Come

A different way to track your progress is by looking at how far you are from the starting point. Carl is a 24-year-old who has begun a possibly successful online company. His vision is to be the next Amazon.com. Yes, that seems impossible or at least many years away. Knowing he hasn't become Amazon yet is not a way to measure for progress. It is far enough in the future that you can't see what path is going to lead to his result.

Carl should concentrate on what he has accomplished so far. He started off sitting at his dining room table. Now he has his own office space. He has customers. He has a business that works. There is money in his bank account, and he is pulling in a profit. He needs to measure his progress on how far he has come and not on how far he must go. Carl can see his has made a lot of momentum and can be sure it will continue to unfold as more milestones get added to his list.

Measuring the Distance to Your Goal

There will come the point where your goal is going to be within your reach. At this point, you can begin to measure how far you are away from reaching that goal. You can now concentrate on getting that gap closed.

Be careful and don't do this too soon. You could hurt your morale. If you continuously ask yourself if you are there yet, you could give your soul a burst of inadequacy. When you are in a marathon, you get a surge of energy when you realize you are just a few feet from finishing. You see a large barrel of ice cream waiting for you at the finish line. Before you know it, you are bursting across the finish line. Once you have reached the halfway mark, begin to measure your progress by how fast you are achieving your goal. Keep that barrel of ice cream in mind and make new goals to push you those last few feet.

A great way to do this is to create a checklist of what you must do to reach this goal. These can be things like running tests with focus groups or writing an email asking for participants. When you have your plan on paper, finishing this project might seem a bit more doable because the steps you need are right in front of you. Even if you do some things wrong, just plan to get you energized and motivated.

Measure Again and Again

Self-Discipline

When you know the way to track your progress and the different progress you should follow, you now need to figure out how often you will monitor your progress. Tracking your progress just one time every week might be plenty. It might be better to track your progress every two or three days.

By doing this, if you realize that you aren't at where you need to be, you will only have to do a couple days work to catch up. If you just check one time each week, you might get a whole week behind before you realize anything is wrong. What you measure, you can manage. Everyone loves to maintain progress. Each day concentrate on measuring your progress goals instead of your outcome goals. Now, pick a less frequent measurement that you can base on where you are currently at in your project like the distance you have left to your goal or the length you have come from the starting point. With some experiments, you might find a magical balance that will keep you focused.

Chapter 13:
Don't Weigh Pros and Cons

Here is a great way to make hard decisions: find all the evidence about possible outcomes, look at the cons and pros, rationally weigh all these factors, and then make your final decision.

This sounds very straightforward, but anyone that has wrestled with significant decisions that are full of complications found that it isn't that easy. Why? The main reason why is because our brains aren't built to think rationally.

Human psychology is full of shortcuts and biases that help us make decisions quickly. Just like our ancestors had to survive thousands of years ago. When talking about more complex dilemmas now, these cognitive quirks can trip us up.

It is in our nature to get overly obsessed about all the negative things in life. Humans are bad at figuring out cons and pros. Negativity always bothers us more.

Self-Discipline

Let's look at it this way; you might be the hiring manager at your job. You have been given the task of hiring a new employee. You've interviewed several people and decide to make a list about their negative and positive qualities. Even if you come up with both negative and positives that are equally compelling and relevant, negatives will always carry more weight.

You are going on vacation and are trying to find a hotel to stay at. You have narrowed it down to three possibilities. One hotel has all the amenities you are looking for but has gotten a few negative reviews from people who have stayed there. These negative reviews fill our minds full of doubt. Even if there are more positive reviews, it won't make you rethink your lousy opinion.

Advertisers have used this trick for a long time. They have realized that showing some doubt about competitors could lead customers to doubt their competitor's products and they will no longer buy their products. When making life decisions, this negative bias isn't going to be useful.

How do we fix this cons and pros list? How can we get around this built-in quirk? The first step is to just know that it exists. You can resolve your internal conflicts faster and act quicker by realizing that negative information will always outweigh the positive.

Stephen Patterson

When looking through hotels and you read one comment about how dirty the hotel was, don't let this one comment cause you to doubt your thoughts about how good this hotel will be for your vacation. Remember to look at your cons and pros list again and this time, move your finger onto the side of the positive.

When you can mentally lower how significant the negatives are and bring the pros into the picture more, you will correct your natural negative bias and will be able to make better choices.

Chapter 14:
Keeping Your End in Mind

This just means when you begin something, you need to have a clear picture of what you want and what steps you need to take to get there. If you are always busy, you should do what is important to you.

The basic principle behind it is that things get created twice. The first time is when you create it in your mind. The second is when you do it. Studies that have been done about the Reticular Activating System say that when you can see your goals and are aware of them, your entire energy and talents get activated so you can develop them.

This concept can be used in many areas and contexts in your life such as personal productivity, sports competition, project management, entrepreneurship, and leadership. Coaches will teach athletes to visualize a successful result during an event before they begin the match. If you know how to successfully complete a project, you can plan it out, communicate the idea to other people, and you can measure the success when it gets finished. You are going to have the right motivation to tackle the whole project.

It is imperative that you can visualize a way to plan projects. To access the unconscious and conscious resources that are available to you, you must have a clear picture of what success will look like. There are six steps to help you evaluate your daily progress:

- First one is life. You need to know what your purpose in life is.

- You need to know what your vision is for the next three to five years.

- You need to know what your goals are for the next one to two years.

- You must know what you are responsible for: health, family, job, career, etc.

- What are your current projects?

- What actions are you currently taking?

Things won't happen just because you thought of them. If you just visualize without acting on it, you are only dreaming. Your vision needs to be supported by strategies or plans that will address it adequately.

Self-Discipline

So, what is your vision in life? The easiest way to get a clear picture is to write down your personal mission statement. Make sure you are clear about whom you want to be, the way you want to live, and the things that give your life meaning.

Conclusion

You now have the tools you need to create healthy habits and stick to your goals to become a successful person. Self-discipline is something so many people are missing, but it is essential to make sure you achieve your dreams. Start creating new habits and get rid of your old bad habits and you're sure to see positive changes in your life.

If you find this book helpful in anyway a review to support my endeavors is much appreciated.

Mental Toughness Mindset

Develop an Unbeatable Mind, Self-Discipline, Iron Will, Confidence, Will Power - Achieve the Success of Sports Athletes, Trainers, Navy SEALs, Leaders and Become Unstoppable

Stephen Patterson

Stephen Patterson

Introduction

Have you ever wondered what sets the best of the best apart from the rest? The truth is it isn't that they are stronger, smarter or more capable, it's that they have a unique mindset that encourages them not to give up, regardless of the adversity.

While this mindset is innate in some people, the rest of us are still in luck as it is also something that can be learned. As such, the following chapters will provide you with everything you need to know in order to instill yourself with the essence of the champion's mind. You will learn to hone aspects of yourself including your self-confidence, self-discipline, attitude, emotional control, leadership, emotional intelligence, your ability to remain in control regardless of the situation, your ability to tune in to your intuition, your overall mental fortitude, your assertiveness and your ability to set and follow through on goals.

Chapter 1:
Discover the Champion Mindset

As children, some people are told they excel in certain subjects while others are told that they succeeded because they tried hard and that effort leads to success. The first group of children can be expected to develop a fixed mindset whereby their brains become more active when they are being told how well they have done. The second group of children can be said to have a growth mindset wherein their minds are the most active when they are learning what they could do better next time. Those with a fixed mindset tend to worry more about how they are seen by others than what they are learning which is why those with a growth mindset tend to be more successful in the long run.

Fixed Mindset
- Wants to look smart or competent regardless of the reality
- Quick to avoid challenges
- Easily thwarted by obstacles

- Thinks effort is "pointless"

- Ignores feedback

- Can feel threatened by the success of others

Growth Mindset
- More interested in long-term results.

- Enjoys a challenge.

- Learns from obstacles

- Equates effort with success

- Appreciates criticism

- Finds inspiration in the success of others

The two mindsets also manifest themselves differently when it comes to dealing with setbacks. When those who have a fixed mindset are met with a setback it directly affects how they see themselves because it shakes their belief in their innate talent. This makes it easier for them to give up on something they are struggling with as they can easily tell themselves that it is just not a talent that is in their wheelhouse. On the other hand, when a person with a growth mindset is met with a challenge, they instead worry about the best way to overcome it and treat the issue as an opportunity to learn and grow.

Those with a fixed mindset believe themselves to have a set level of ability which means that if they cannot surpass an obstacle on the first try, there is no reason for them to try again because nothing about the scenario will ever change. It doesn't take much to see how this type of reductive mindset can make it difficult to start working your way out of a difficult situation as it can make it seem like there is no point in even getting started. On the other hand, those with a growth mindset always appreciate a good challenge for the opportunity to overcome it and learn from the experience.

Change your mind: In order to change your personal outlook, you will need to learn to take advantage of the brain's neuroplasticity. Years ago, it was thought that the brain only developed during childhood. However, modern studies have discovered and proven that the brain does not lose its ability to program itself, even in adulthood. It simply takes more effort when it happens later in life, but it is, nonetheless, still possible. Studies show that not only can the brain be programmed in its thinking, but even the physical structure of the brain will change in the process of learning new information and behaviors.

Stephen Patterson

In order to go from a fixed to a growth mindset, the first thing that you are going to want to do is to take an analytical look at your life and see which habits you currently take for granted are enabling this destructive mindset to perpetuate itself. Once you have really looked at how you act daily it will be much easier to determine how you can counteract them for the better. The easiest way to get started is through a dedicated diet of repetition.

Changing your mindset is all about committing to the task at hand and changing small thoughts regarding your ability to change in general. Over time, you will be able to consciously alter larger thoughts which will then make it easier to take more active control over your mindset.

When working to keep a growth mindset in all things, it is important to keep it up even when the going gets tough. It will likely seem like the easiest thing in the world to do while things are going well, but a fixed mindset is much more likely to manifest itself during times when roadblocks begin presenting themselves. Your fixed mindset will likely make you want to abandon all hope of forward progress when these roadblocks appear.

In this case, it is important to try to stop thinking of the challenges as roadblocks and start thinking of them as opportunities for you to learn and grow. Finding personal ways to meet the challenges that come your way head on without dwelling on them unnecessarily is the first step towards making a real change for the better.

Once you have begun to change your faulty habits it is important to have a broad understanding of how long the change will take. The easier the bad habit is to engage in the more difficult it will be to change which is why having a general idea of the timetable for such can make working through it much easier. During this time, it will also be important to make a mental list of places or activities which trigger the bad habit and avoid them when at all possible. Finding yourself in a situation where you are face to face with the things which trigger your bad habit is a surefire way to slip up and fall back into old habits.

Making the extra effort to ensure that you remain motivated no matter how long the process takes is no easy feat, but you should find that keeping your eye on the end goal will make the entire process seem that much easier. Then, after a timeline has been established in regard to how long it will likely take for you to form your new habits you will want to add in smaller milestones that you can look forward to in order to prove to yourself that you are making progress, regardless of what the moment to moment might feel like. Keep in mind that even the most complicated habits rarely take more than 10 weeks to form which means that if you are having trouble getting something to stick then you may have simply not been trying for long enough.

Be grateful: While making a concentrated effort to be more grateful might seem like an odd way to improve your mindset, studies show that this feeling is linked to additional feelings related to an overall improved quality of life, less stress and even less pronounced signs of aging. In fact, those with a more grateful attitude are also known to have a lower average blood pressure and lower overall levels of aggression as well. As such, if you make it a point to start each day off gratefully then developing a more grateful attitude, in general, will happen as a result. In order to jumpstart the process, consider the following tips.

Writing a handwritten letter to a friend or loved one to thank them for a recent act of kindness will not only make their day, but it will also help you to get in the habit of being grateful for the little things in life. It is important that this letter is handwritten as it makes the entire act less spontaneous and more focused. Taking the extra time will also make it easy for you to reflect on what it is you are truly grateful for.

Along similar lines, you may also find it useful to purchase a physical calendar and write five things you are thankful for on it every day for a year. Not only will doing so help you always go a long way towards being grateful, but it will also make it easy to find inspiration during times when you otherwise feel as though you don't have anything to be grateful for.

You should also get into the habit of thinking about every experience you have each day as its own type of gift. Make a concentrated effort for a week to thank the universe each day for the things you regularly enjoy but frequently accept without thinking twice about them. Thank the universe for a beautiful sunrise, your morning tea or even the challenges you face throughout the day. After you spend a week or more focusing on being grateful for the little things you will find that you are more grateful in general without even thinking twice about it.

You may also want to consider what major events you have coming up in the relatively near future so that you can spend some time each day focusing on how grateful you are that this thing is going to come to pass and that you get to enjoy it. When the first event does come to fruition, don't rest on your laurels and instead pick another activity or event that you can be grateful for soon and start the process all over again.

Chapter 2:
Improve Your Self-Confidence

Building self-confidence is a dream that many people have, yet it is something that few pursue. This is because, like anything worth doing, getting started building self-confidence can be quite difficult especially if you have very little of it to begin with. Regardless of your current level of self-confidence, however, there are several simple yet productive thought exercises you can practice forcing your mind into the habit of thinking about things in the proper self-confident light.

Building self-confidence is a dream that many people have, yet it is something that few pursue. This is because, like anything worth doing, getting started building self-confidence can be quite difficult especially if you have very little of it to begin with. Regardless of your current level of self-confidence, however, there are several simple yet productive thought exercises you can practice forcing your mind into the habit of thinking about things in the proper self-confident light.

Think About Where Your Fears Actually Come From

When it comes time to assert yourself, if you find yourself becoming afraid, instead, you must first force yourself to understand that the only way this fear will ever leave you is if you master it completely. If you're still having trouble, consider the following tips for success:

Reframe your anxiety: If you are uncertain about the outcome of an event, that uncertainty can manifest itself as anticipation which is just a hair's breadth from fear. Reacting in a scenario that would benefit from self-confidence with anxiety instead, will destroy any momentum that you may have previously developed.

As such, you may find it helpful to react to your anxiety as if it were curiosity. Instead of being anxious about an outcome you can instead trick your mind into being curious as to the results instead. Curiosity and self-confidence go together much more easily than anxiety and self-confidence and you may find that curiously helps your confident momentum continue.

Take the time to decide why you are afraid: If you find yourself always responding to situations that require self-confidence in the same fearful pattern. Consider this, the human mind loves to find patterns, even when no true pattern exists. This means you may be responding to an established pattern and not actually the specifics of the current situation.

Stephen Patterson

Think about the what could really happen: Another reason that many people find themselves unable to exercise self-confidence in social situations is that they let their minds get out of control when it comes to considering all the possible things that could go wrong in a given situation. While considering all the options isn't inherently a bad thing, the fact of the matter is that most of these worse-case scenarios are extremely unlikely to ever come true. Instead of letting your mind get carried away, a better course of action is to look at the situation a second time as a means of determining if things are as terrible as they first appeared. Nine times out of ten you are going to discover that the truth is far more manageable than the initial round of possibilities that you came up with.

While you might find it difficult to conceive of a world where whatever minor social faux pas you have committed is not the object of ridicule by those around you, the simple truth is that most people are too wrapped up in their own problems to worry about whatever it is that you are doing. While the moment where you try and fail may be burned into your brain, odds are no one else will even remember it tomorrow. Remember, you don't need to be on guard against failure, it is a part of life; what you do need to be on guard against is apathy that makes you reject the notion of getting back up and trying again.

Don't Just Think About It

While thinking about how you are going to be more confident in the future is easy, it won't do much for you when it comes to taking actions that are perceived as confident by those around you. Unfortunately, taking those steps is much more difficult than simply thinking about them and the only thing that mitigates this is the fact that stepping out of your comfort zone for the first time is tricky, and potentially terrifying for everyone who first sets out to try it. The good news is that if you persevere it will get easier every time you do it.

To help you to get over the initial hump, consider the following:

Refocus: Whenever you find yourself hesitating prior to being confident in any situation, the first thing you should do before shying away is to give yourself an extra moment to think it through. Think about how being confident in the given situation would dramatically improve the circumstances you currently find yourself in and how much better your life would then be because of it. Furthermore, consider how much better your life would be if you approached every single situation in this confident manner. While this little boost of persuasion might not seem like much on paper, in practice you will be surprised at just how effective it can be. Give it a try for a few weeks and you will be well on your way to building a confident habit.

Don't worry about the consequences: The thing that trips up many people when they are trying to be confident is thinking too much about the potential negative consequences that could come about from a confident action. They end up stuck in their own heads, unable to make any move and the time for confidence passes them by. One of the quickest ways to mitigate this problem is to simply act confidently first before your brain can muster up a reason to talk you down. When you find yourself approaching a scenario where you would benefit from being confident, act first and think later, you can worry about what happens next later.

Love Yourself

When it comes to being confident in who you are, a big part of that is learning to truly accept yourself for who you are and all the various weaknesses or strengths that go into that. While it may seem basic, the truth of the matter is that a good round of self-analysis will make finding the self-confidence and even the personal empowerment you are looking for much easier to find.

A good way to go about taking an accurate count of what you are working with is to start by standing in front of a large mirror and then disrobing so that you are standing in front of yourself completely naked. While this might sound extreme, it is important to go through with it and really look at what it is you are looking at. Most people have a dramatically different view of themselves in their minds compared to the reality and this is a chance to ensure your expectations are completely aligned with reality. It is important to consider both the areas that you traditionally consider your strengths, as well as your weaknesses and to really drink it all in. You don't need to necessarily enjoy everything you see; you just need to have a clear and honest picture of the truth in your mind.

If you come across numerous flaws in this area that you feel are completely unacceptable, the best course of action is likely going to be taking it upon yourself to ensure those flaws will not bother you in the future. Regardless if this means cutting out a few favorite foods you overindulge in from time to time or if it means starting a complete diet and exercise overhaul, you will be surprised at making a positive change when it comes to taking care of yourself can make it easier to be more confident and self-empowered almost right from the start.

Consider how you feel about perfection: No one, not even the most confident person you know, can be perfect all the time. This is a fact that everyone knows but few people believe. It is easy to only view others, especially those who embody traits we envy, as never failing at anything they try while at the same time ballooning our own imperfections to extreme proportions. In these situations, it is important to remember that the mind is more likely to remember our own mistakes than those of others which means the things we don't even remember happening to others may well be enough to cause them to have their own issues with confidence. If this is the case, then it also means that they do not remember our own mistakes with any clarity so we should not focus on them as much either.

Don't compare yourself to others: Comparing yourself to those who seem to embody all the traits that you covet is an unhealthy exercise that will only produce biased results. Unless you are intimately familiar with the person you are comparing yourself to, the odds are good that you are only seeing one side of the story. You might be seeing that other person only at their best with no possible way of understanding their own struggles and personal roadblocks. What's more, any problems you are aware of will seem more minor than your own due to perception bias. The next time you go to compare yourself to someone else, stop. Take that time to come up with a few reasons to appreciate yourself instead.

Confidence in Action

After you begin to feel more confident, the next step is to learn to express it appropriately. With practice, you will find that speaking up for yourself in verbal and physical situations will allow you to find out more about how to project your confidence. How you interact with those around you is a clear representation of how confident you feel. Your goal should be to be protective of your rights and the rights of those around you while at the same time not being overly aggressive and forcing others to do things, they are not comfortable with.

It is important to know when to speak up in social situations, especially if your level of self-confidence has yet to improve very far. Failing to speak up when you are otherwise entitled to reinforce negative thought patterns including projecting negative thoughts and looking for approval in others and modifying your own needs to suit other people. It is important to always stand up for yourself as this shows others that you are a valuable and worthwhile person who deserves to be treated as such.

When asserting yourself it is important to do so appropriately and to give yourself a moment to prepare before jumping right in. It is important to take the time to ensure that you are in the right when it comes to a perceived slight and after that to gather your energy and your thoughts for the coming confrontation. If you are approaching another person, it is important to use authoritative body language. Hold your head up high, keep your back straight, let your arms hang naturally and set your feet firmly a moderate distance apart.

As you approach the other person, it is important to always speak in a clear and assertive tone that is commanding but not haughty. You want to project the fact that you are in control of the situation because you are self-confident, not conceited.

This means you will want to walk with a straight back and your head held high. When you stand in front of the other person you are going to want to square your feet and your shoulders and let your arms naturally hang at your sides. When you speak, make sure to make eye contact with the other person and avoid crossing your arms at all costs as this is often considered a sign of weakness.

Speak your mind: When you do talk to the other party you are going to want to ensure that you use a voice that is calm but still authoritative and a little bit quitter than your normal speaking voice. Making the other person strain to hear you is a power play as it means they automatically must let you control the situation in order to know what is going on. The tone that you use is extremely important as it needs to make the other person believe that obeying you is the logical choice of action. Making it clear to other people that you are confident is all about letting them know that you are in control of the current situation. When you start speaking you want to make it clear what your issue is and then follow up directly with how you plan to rectify it, so the conversation starts with all the elements clearly laid on the table.

During this discussion, it is important to keep in mind that your end goal should not be to ensure that you win out at the expense of anyone else involved, being self-confident doesn't mean always getting your way; it is more about directing the conversation in a way that solves the initial issue in the most effective way possible.

Chapter 3:
Improve Your Self-Discipline

When it comes to achieving the goals and happiness that you want out of life, there is one simple thing you can do that will increase your chances of success 10-fold: improve your self-discipline. While the requirements to achieve your goals will vary based on the specifics, they will all have one thing in common, dedication and hard work will get you there, and self-discipline will make it possible.

Studies show that the more self-discipline and self-control a person has, the happier that person is as they tend to feel as though they are generally more prepared for anything that life can throw at them. This is because, while those without self-discipline spend time motivating themselves to do things, those with self-discipline simply did them which makes them more productive overall.

While those who lack self-discipline likely think that it is an innate behavior, in all actuality it is a skill which means that like any skill it can be improved with practice over time. There are a number of ways that you can strengthen your resolve and improve your ability to maintain your self-discipline even when it may seem difficult or impossible to do so; first, however, you must understand that it is up to you, and no one else, to make better choices in the first place. Your future self is directly influenced by what you choose to do in the present, do yourself a favor and choose wisely.

When it comes to exercising your self-discipline, especially in a scenario that will require significant time and energy to completely successfully, it is completely natural for your mind to come up with excuses as to why it makes sense to take the easy way out, some of them might even be rather believable. If you find that you are regularly putting off various tasks because of a fear of overexerting yourself, due to external factors or because you simply have too much on your plate then you may need to reevaluate your schedule and see what is really important to you before moving forward.

Internal motivation: If you hope to someday to use your self-discipline to do great things then it is important you work to foster the type of mental fortitude that will make it possible for you to treat it like a job at all times. Being your own boss means that there will never be anyone looking over your shoulder or forcing you to get to work when there are things that you would rather be doing instead. Rather, that motivation to succeed will need to come from within and will need to motivate you to do what you need to do day in and day out. Only by fueling your personal drive for success will you be able to improve and stick with it even when the going gets tough. Self-discipline isn't something that can be used halfway, you either can keep yourself in check or you don't, there is no room for middle ground.

Commit completely: When you start out down the path to self-discipline it is important to dedicate yourself to the admittedly monumental task ahead of you. Commit to the idea fully and without reservation as once you do the day to day interactions you must undertake to pursue your chosen course of action become much easier. Try making a promise on something you hold dear or even just yourself, whatever it may be; by dedicating yourself to the task at hand will make it that much easier to drown out any voices of dissension or excuses your mind might put forth to allow you an easy out from your goal. If you do not commit completely you run the risk of giving up and returning to negative habits and losing months or even years of work.

Understand your weaknesses: Everyone has common triggers that lead to negative behaviors especially those opposed to a highly self-disciplined lifestyle. When first starting out with the goal of improving your self-discipline it can be helpful to look inward and make a list of what you want to change and the items, settings or activities that trigger the negative behaviors you wish to change. While it can be difficult to confront yourself so bluntly all at once, looking at what you need to change will make it easier to establish ways to change it.

Practice makes perfect: If you feel that you will have an especially hard time deviating from a negative habit or routines, it can be helpful to try avoiding whatever it may be for a short period of time to allow yourself the opportunity to know what fully committing to a more self-disciplined lifestyle will be like thus allowing you to prepare for its effects beforehand. While a practice session can be beneficial, if you allow it to turn into several such sessions then you are just prolonging the negative habit.

Keep an eye out for triggers: When it comes to getting in the habit of practicing self-discipline, it is critical that you take the time early on to consider the types of things that commonly trigger you to lose control. Getting a better handle on your triggers will make it easier to understand the underlying habits they prop up, which will make it easier for you to avoid the whole affair in the future. While you might not be able to think of any triggers right away, if you keep the topic on your mind, then as you go through your week you should notice things that are more likely to stray from the chosen path.

Removing triggers: Once you have managed to make a list of your triggers, the next thing you are going to want to do is everything in your power to ensure you remove them from your general line of sight until you have your habit of being self-disciplined down pat. While you will rarely be able to remove absolutely all the power a given trigger has, you should be able to lessen it significantly, with practice. It is important to keep in mind that the early days are likely going to be tough going, but each time you withstand a serious temptation it will get a little easier.

Build a routine: Regardless of your self-discipline goals, if you aren't already maintaining a schedule where you can eat regularly, then it is important to make doing so a priority. Not only will eating at regular periods help you to feel better, but it will also ensure that your brain has the fuel required to make good decisions. Specifically, studies show that those with low blood sugar are three times more likely to make poor decisions based on a lack of resolve than those whose blood sugar was on point.

Scheduling (writing down a list): Perhaps the most important thing to do in taking control of your free time is to take stock of exactly how much you have and divide it up accordingly by writing it out. This might seem obvious, but I can't tell you how many people I know that just have their schedule inside their head and still expect to get everything done. People are prone to forget things, and I hate to break it to those of you who think you can reach maximum productivity this way, but I promise you, sooner or later you too will forget something you otherwise would've remembered had you written it down.

And no, you don't always need to keep a notepad and pencil on you, because you know that smartphone of yours? Yeah, the one that's either within arm's reach from you right now, or possibly the thing you're using to read this book with? Well, that thing isn't only a powerful tool to stay connected to the things and people you need connection with; it's also your very own personal assistant that can aid you in making great use of the free time you have so you can start making strides in what you want to accomplish.

All you need to do is open a blank document or list app every Sunday night – or before whichever day you want your week to start – and title it: To-Do This Week. Then, simply, write down what it is you want to accomplish that week.

- Exercise

- Start planning that trip

- Declutter the apartment and put some things on Craigslist

- Etc.

Don't make excuses: When you first set out to reach your goal, it is perfectly natural for your mind to start putting up roadblocks to all your new hard work in the form actions that are more immediately gratifying instead. While these alternatives might be gratifying in the short-term, they are not going to be nearly as satisfying in the long-term as succeeding at your dream of becoming famous would be.

It is important to understand that while it is easy to give into the short-term satisfaction now, you are sure to regret it later when the minor happiness from distraction dissipates and you are still no closer to achieving anything that will measurably increase the quality of your life as a whole. If you just can't seem to get your mind to fall in line, then you may find success with the concept of bargaining, which can help to keep things in check until your self-discipline has properly developed.

For example, if you feel as though you could be more physically fit but are having a hard time exercising as much as you know you should because you are constantly making excuses as to why you can't start your YouTube channel, then you can bargain with yourself to get yourself going and building positive habits. You could set up a reward system for yourself, and essentially train your brain the way you would a puppy. As time goes on, and you start to see serious results, then you won't need to use the bargaining system anymore as the results will speak for themselves.

If bargaining doesn't work, then you may find better success by making a concentrated effort to change the excuses that your mind is coming up with. Rather than telling yourself that it's okay and that you can always start tomorrow, get tough with yourself and blame the true source of the problem for the issues you are facing getting started.

Make a wholehearted commitment: One of the biggest keys to self-discipline is having a commitment to your goal. This gives you the biggest reason to keep pushing on if you can hold yourself accountable. If you can't then you will find that it is hard to hold on to your commitment, which can cause some problems.

You can make a personal commitment, or you can make a public commitment. While a public commitment may seem like it is the easiest to keep, that may not be the truth. Often, those around us may find themselves discouraging us from achieving our goals due to a feeling of inadequacy amongst themselves. It is much easier to keep a personal commitment because you will be able to build yourself up, rather than depending on others to build you up instead.

Committing yourself to your goal does not mean you will automatically succeed though. You must have a more detailed commitment than "I will get this done."

You must commit yourself not only to your goal, but to doing what it takes to achieve your goal and to finding the steps that you can take to make achieving your goal that much more possible. If you are not committing yourself fully, then you may not make your goal.

Commit yourself to consistency. You must be consistent in your daily habit changes to achieve your goal. If you lack consistency, it is so much easier to fall back into your old ways than it is to keep yourself moving towards your goal.

Critical Thinking Steps for Improved Self-Discipline

Problem Identification: Your first task in critical thinking is figuring out whether there is a problem at the current moment. At times, when you must figure this out, you might realize that there isn't an actual problem, only a simple mistake or misunderstanding going on. If you decide that there is a problem now, the next step is determining what the issue is. The ability to look at the positives and negatives and state and define the issue is a mark of high intelligence.

Analyzing the Issue: Next, you need to consider the issue from every angle possible. Can you solve this problem? Is it a concrete issue or mostly in our own mind? Can you do this on your own or will you be needing assistance from other people? At times, assessing the situation from various perspectives will lead to an easy and obvious resolution for the issue. In addition, it could help you realize your own biases in the situation.

List Possible Answers: Now, you should do some brainstorming and think of a few different solutions to the issue. There are many different answers for each problem. List any solution that you come up with and then try to narrow down each possibility at the end of this practice. When you have more than one possible solution, you increase your chances of finding the right one.

Choose a Solution: Next, you should select the solution that appears to apply best to this situation you're in. Various situations will require different answers to the issue. A lot of times, what will solve one situation, won't apply to another one that is similar. Figure out which will work for your current problem. Do this only after you have given this plenty of thought and can make an informed and intelligent decision on the matter.

Chapter 4:
Improve Your Attitude

People with low self-esteem tend to wallow in negativity. By focusing on the negative, you ignore large amounts of information that might otherwise make you feel better about yourself. Healthy self-esteem is the goal here. There is a sea of difference between, "I really need to be more physically active" than "I am a lazy blob." Excessive self-loathing can heavily backfire because it shifts the focus from ways through which one can improve on their failures.

Over a longer period, negative self-speak can up your stress level, and lead to major depression. Learning to tame negative self-talk is the key to overcoming challenges, feeling more confident and achieving the life of your dreams. If you have struggled with self-esteem for some time, chances are that you often overlook the positive aspects of your life. Positivity is powerful; this chapter will provide suggestions for harnessing its powers in order to go through life with better self-esteem.

Positive Self-Talk: Self-talk is the interactions that you have with the voice that resides inside of your own mind. The things that this voice says greatly affect the way that you feel and think. As such, negative self-talk can lead to saddening thought patterns and a lack of self-esteem. Consequently, positive self-talk is an essential component in building up one's self-esteem.

Making the practice of positive self-talk a regular habit should be your goal in terms of self-talk outcomes. Practicing positive self-talk might feel unusual or funny when you first begin, but, after you start to benefit from its self-esteem boosting effects, you will yearn for the opportunity to engage in positive self-talk uninterrupted.

Positive self-talk does not necessarily involve pointing out the things that you wish to change. For example, you might tell yourself that you want to behave less erratically, experience fewer feelings of anxiety, and stop living in a messy apartment. However, the problem with these thoughts lies in the fact that they focus on what you would rather not have. Instead, positive self-talk should focus on the things and outcomes that you do indeed want.

Positive self-talk takes place in the present-tense and affirms the qualities that correlate with high self-esteem. For example, repeat to yourself affirmations like "I am assertive," "I can make as much money as I want to," and "I feel calm."

Throw negative self-talk into a box: Visualize your mistakes in a tiny box the next time you find yourself exaggerating each of them. For instance, if you find yourself underperforming at a meeting or presentation, rather than thinking, it's the end of your career, try rationalizing by criticizing your choice of words. "I could have used better words, or my choice of words wasn't up to the mark." This really sounds more believable than "I screwed up my career." Visualize a small box and put your poor choice of words into it. You will subconsciously diminish the problem's size and end up feeling way more confident.

Practice possibility thinking: If you are constantly thinking in extremely glowing terms, you may trigger the mental lie detector which tells you that you are functioning in a surreal world. Do not force yourself to resort to extremely unreal positive thoughts. Instead, take a neutral approach when you are besieged with negative thoughts. Be more neutral in your thinking. Think about possibilities why a certain thing could have occurred. When you feel heavy and low on energy, instead of saying, "I am a fleshy seal or fat cow" or even, "I am a goddess or diva, irrespective of how I look" try saying, "I'd be really nice if I can knock off a few pounds. It will make me feel healthier, more energetic and fitter." We've taken a more middle and neutral ground here since changing negative to positive self-talk quickly can be highly unrealistic. Adopt a more realistic, practical and gradual approach.

Affirmations: Emotions that feed a negative attitude are triggered by the way you perceive situations that you have previously been in and those that are on the horizon. These perceptions are, in turn, influenced by the filters that your mind has built up over time based on the data it has recorded from the experiences you have had. When you find yourself thinking through this type of negative filter you will likely only see the negative aspects of a given situation, regardless of the positive ones that existed at the same time. If you chronically see every glass as half empty, then you may have an issue with negative filters.

In fact, if your attitude gets bad enough, your filters will likely go so far as to remove all of the calming and positive aspects of your day so all you can see are the things that make you unhappy, compounding the problem and making it seem as though there is no way to solve it. This is where affirmations and mantras come in as the repetition that comes along with them is a great way to bypass these filters and allow your mind to let in some new thoughts for a change.

An affirmation is simply a positive sentence that you write down multiple times throughout the day. A mantra is the same sentence, just repeated in your mind instead of written down. They are both a great way to quiet the mental background noise that is created by your anxiety and to eventually retrain your brain, bypassing the existing mental filters in the process.

- Examples include:
- *Today, you are perfect*
- *Forward progress! Just keep moving!*
- *You are the sky*
- *I am attracting all the love I dream of and deserve*
- *Follow my path to happiness*
- *I am strong. I am beautiful. I am enough*
- *I am grateful for my life so far and for what is to come*
- *I am fulfilled*

Consider core beliefs: If you have been dealing with a negative outlook for most of your life, then it is possible that there are facets of your core belief system that may ultimately end up being incompatible with the way the world works. The first step in getting past this issue is to determine the mental agreements that are coming into play so that you can correct them and move forward in a more effective fashion. These mental agreements often come in bundles which means if you can find the package of beliefs that are being affected, you will be on the right track.

As with many of the exercises discussed in this book, it can be difficult to get started with this exercise, but if you keep it up you will find that it gets much easier with practice. The best way to get started is going to be by working to uncover the core belief that is giving you the most trouble now. You can think of uncovering this core belief as solving a mystery which means you need to look for clues that are left in place by your subconscious.

Therefore, it is so important to distinguish these types of thoughts from actual core beliefs as your thoughts are rarely to be trusted if you are dealing with an extremely entrenched negative attitude. When it comes to tracking down a core belief now, the best way is to follow the trail of emotions you are having in response to an event. You will want to continue to question your specific emotions and the ways in which they are being externally influenced in order to get to the core beliefs that are pulling the strings.

Learn to properly manage rejection: It can be easy to get discouraged in the face of adversity, which is why it can be so effective to cognitively refrain the situation by putting the issue into perspective in the grand scheme of things. Most things are going to become infinitely unimportant over time which is why this can be such an effective strategy, especially for those things that really seem like they are the end of the world now. What's more, by looking at things for a more manageable angle you may even find a way to turn the issue around now that you previously hadn't considered.

Find the good in every situation: While you may have heard this advice before, rather than taking it as a general admonition to be positive you should think of it more as a thought exercise. Specifically, task yourself with finding something positive in every situation, regardless of how hopeless it might seem on the surface and then don't stop thinking about it until you have come up with a reason that holds at least a little water. If you can manage to find the good in situations that tax your mental and physical endurance to the ultimate test, then the rest should be easy.

One useful way of going about doing so is by finding the humor hiding in even the most trying and darkest situations. Try and crack a joke or, at the very least, remind yourself that it is sure to make a good story at some point in the future. Alternately, you can counter the grim prospect of the darkest timeline by putting an absurdist bent on the whole affair. For example, if you find out you are being laid off at the end of the week, then you can focus on figuring out the most absurd things you can do with your final days or the outlandish jobs you could pursue next.

Kriya: A kriya is a precise sequence of exercises that are used to reach a specific goal. The kriya for abdominal strength is a mixture of breathing exercises and precise movements that are designed to strengthen the core while also teaching you to find the internal strength required to turn your back on your bad habits. Furthermore, it is also known to power up the third chakra in a way that is commonly thought to serve as a starting point for future feelings of transformation and empowerment. Once you have finished this kriya, it is likely that you will feel more balanced, grounded and generally at one with the universe.

If you plan on starting off with this kriya then you are going to want to ensure you can commit to doing it every single day for 40 days. This is how long it will take for your brain to start forming the types of pathways that you should be aiming for as they will be free of the bad habits that you were previously cultivating.

You start this meditative exercise by lying on your back with your legs stretched out straight and your arms at your sides. You can also place them beneath your lower back if you need additional support in that area. Once you are in the position you will then want to inhale slowly while at the same time flexing your core while you slowly lift your right leg into the air until it is perpendicular to the floor. You are going to want to breathe in while getting into this position, hold it for a few seconds and then exhale as you slowly return it to the ground. You will then want to repeat the same steps for the other leg before repeating the process for a total of three minutes.

Chapter 5:
Improve Your Control of Negative Emotions

Cognitive Behavioral Therapy, more commonly known as CBT, is a type of therapy that works around the assumption that there are simply some behaviors that cannot be controlled through conscious thought alone. In fact, it posits that all behaviors occur thanks to a mixture of internal and external stimuli and a lifetime of conditioning in one an infinite number of ways.

While it was first created to help those with depression deal with their condition, this type of psychotherapy has become a popular way of dealing with a wide variety of issues including anger and anxiety as well. At its heart, however, its primary goal is to help users mitigate problems they are having directly by finding their associated negative behaviors and any associated thoughts and then changing them into something more beneficial. CBT is a mixture of behavioral therapy and cognitive therapy and thus makes use of the guiding principles of each.

Stephen Patterson

While the techniques discussed in this will be more effective if you work on them with a therapist who specializes in CBT, you can also find success if you stick with them yourself. When you first begin attempting CBT techniques it is vital that you remember that you are developing a new skill as well. What this means is that, just like any other skill, you are going to have a difficult time of things at first but that things will get easier each day if you keep it up and don't get discouraged. While this is easy to say, it is important to take it to heart as the first time you try many of the exercises in the following chapter you may very well fail which is why having unrealistic expectations up front can make it easier to get back on the horse should the situation arise.

Breathe properly: In many stressful situations, if the mind is feeling overwhelmed, the first thing the body does is alter its breathing. The way you are breathing is essentially the trigger that directly affects everything else the way your body functions. When you receive either to little or too much oxygen it serves to significantly enhance the seriousness of any other symptoms that might be present, making a mild issue into a serious attack in no time flat.

Luckily, learning to control your breathing can be quite straightforward as soon as you start actively thinking about it. The quickest means of doing so is via what is known as the 4/7/8 method. To practice this method all you need to do is find a comfortable place to sit, sit with your shoulders square and your back straight and then breathe in slowly for a total of four seconds. Next, you will want to hold your breath for a total of seven seconds and then breathe out slowly for a total of eight seconds. You will want to repeat this process until the issue resolves itself or you have completed six repetitions for a total of two minutes. You may want to close your eyes as well, to help yourself relax even more.

While you might not notice much of a change at first, over time you will find that when you do this exercise that everything around you begins to slow down, taking your heartbeat with it. If two minutes doesn't seem to be enough for you, then you may want to work up to five minute sessions, or even 10, the important thing is that you find the right amount of focused breathing that works for you so you can bust it out when you need it most.

Progressive muscle relaxation: Progressive muscle relaxation is a technique, like measured breathing, that can be used now to deal with particularly bad anxiety flair ups. It involves tensing and then relaxing specific groups of muscles as a means of distracting your anxiety and short circuiting the loop that causes it to manifest in the first place. This is since it is difficult for your body to maintain a tensed, anxious state, and a relaxed calm state at the same time.

As such, if you feel an anxiety attack coming your way, a period of focused relaxation may be just what you need to cut it off at the pass. You may also find this type of exercise useful if you are having difficulty sleeping.

While you will eventually be able to use this exercise now, while you are still getting the hang of it you are going to want to find some place quiet where you can focus on the task at hand. Give yourself 15 to 20 minutes of practice time to start, though once you get the hang of it you will likely be able to experience the same results in far less time. To start, you simply need to pick a specific part of your body and shift the entirety of your focus to it. This step will be the same regardless of which muscle group you are focusing on.

After you have finished tensing, you will then want to abruptly change course and relax the muscles you were focusing on (in this case your hand). After you have finished tensing you will want to relax those muscles completely, feeling all the tightness float out of your muscles, and from your mental state as well. You will want to go completely limp for this exercise to be effective, before then focusing on the difference between the two states.

Journaling: Your thoughts are a continuous stream; there are no waking moments where you aren't thinking about something. It may not also be in the front of your mind, but thoughts are always present and always moving. As the adage goes, "I think, therefore I am." It's difficult to recognize everything that passes through our heads as it is. Throw anxiety into the mix and it becomes impossible to follow everything.

A journal is a great way to track your anxiety. By putting your thoughts on paper you'll give them tangible form. Though like a diary, an anxiety journal isn't for just a record of your daily happenings. It's closer to an operating table where you'll examine, dissect, and explore your distressing thoughts. This is helpful in several ways:

Better self-expression. How often have you tried to explain your anxiety to someone only to feel like they didn't fully understand what you were saying? It's difficult to articulate worry, especially now. But no one will have a better understanding of your thought processes than you do. By laying it out on the page you can practice how you can communicate it to others. In therapy sessions, you can even read your entries to your therapist.

Self-reflection. As we become more aware of ourselves and our thought cycles it can become easy to let thoughts get lost in the blur. If you have a written record of your thoughts it acts likes a map of sorts. You can see what sort of thoughts you had on any given day and see how they changed overtime, creating pathways and patterns that you can recognize overtime. This recognition will help you develop plans going forward.

Progress. It's also beneficial to have the journal of your thoughts because it shows how much progress you make on your journey to recovery. But of equal value to these positives are seeing where you come up short. You are going to want to use the ABCD model for describing your experiences.

First, you will list the activating event, including an explanation of the situation, with all personal bias removed, this should just state the facts. You will also want to make note of the first thing crossed your mind when the event occurred as this is likely an automatic thought which means knowing it could be useful later. From there, you will want to write down any beliefs that came into play as well, starting with the type of negative thoughts you experienced. If possible, you are also going to want to write down the source of the belief as well.

From there, you are going to want to write down the relevant consequences that occurred from the way you handled the incident, both short and long-term. Finally, if possible, you are going to want to dispute your negative thoughts and replace them with alternatives that you could have used instead. It is important to get into the habit of writing in your journal at the end of every single day.

When dealing with CBT, it is impossible to have too much information about what is going on in your daily life, the more events you write down each day the better. While initially, you may have a difficult time remembering the finer details of the things that happen to you throughout the day, it is important to keep up the practice regardless.

Self-soothing: If you find yourself in a situation with a trigger that you simply cannot abide, and your only option seems to be having a panic or anxiety attack, then you may find it useful to distract yourself with alternative stimuli in order to short circuit the attack and help yourself self-correct. The specifics of what you do to take yourself out of the moment doesn't matter, if it serves to take your mind off the negative emotion that is threatening to spill out.

You can start by doing something as simple as paying attention to what is around you, finding a calm spot to be by yourself temporarily, or even find something shiny to keep yourself entertained until the feeling passes. You may also find listening to music to be effective, getting a massage or even literally stopping to smell the roses. Finding something salty or sugary to eat will also give you a caloric boost that will often serve to get your mind on the right track.

Radical acceptance: Radical acceptance is a healthy alternative to many habitual avoidance techniques that you can use when you come across a situation that, at face value, seems extremely unfair or otherwise completely out of your control. Rather than focusing on this injustice now, you can instead practice accepting the negative situation as a fact and instead focusing your mental efforts on doing everything you can to solve the problem at hand.

It is important to keep in mind that there is a clear difference between accepting something and agreeing or approving of the way in which it is proceeding. Acceptance is the best solution when a situation seems completely beyond your control; for example, if you find out that you did not get the promotion that you were hoping for, an unhealthy, but extremely common, the response is to blame your superiors for their shortsightedness.

Exercise More

Several studies prove that exercise is an effective way to fight negative emotions and other mental disorders like depression, anxiety, and phobias. Exercise can help relieve stress, improves overall mood, improves memory, and increase the amount of quality sleep you get each night. Perspiration releases natural endorphins which are the hormones that make us feel happy and positive. If you haven't exercised in a while, the following set of exercises should allow you to choose a level that's right for you.

10-minute-high intensity workout: You will want to complete the entire circuit three times and take a 10 second rest between each set. Each circuit should take 3 minutes and 10 seconds.

Sumo squats: Start with your feet at slightly more than hip-width apart and keep your toes pointed facing outward at a 45-degree angle. Place all your weight on the heels of your feet, your chest upright and your back straight, lower yourself down towards the ground until your thighs are essentially parallel to the ground. Using your quads and your glutes, push yourself back into the starting position. To end each set, move into a reverse lung and fold your body forward while keeping your arms stretched overhead.

Jumping jacks: Start by standing in a relaxed stance, with your feed about hip-width apart and your arms resting at your sides. Jump up while spreading your feet and raising your arms above your head. Repeat as many times as possible, as quickly as possible, for about 45 seconds.

Jab, cross, front kick (left): Start with your left foot in front of your right foot and your hips facing right. Raise your arms so that you are in somewhat of a boxer stance. Start with a jab by punching forward with your left arm straight out. Move directly into throwing a cross by punching with your left arm and rotating your body to the right.

Stephen Patterson

Chapter 6:
Improve Your Leadership Skills

It is easy to lead; it is difficult to lead well. If you are interested in leading others to the best of their abilities, make sure you strive to always embody the following traits.

Be aware: A good leader understands that there are some inalienable differences between the rank-in-file, middle and senior management, accepts this as fact and acts accordingly. It is important to be aware of how you interact with your team and to always conduct yourself in a way that doesn't suggest superiority but simply allows you to retain an unbiased perspective. This can be a difficult quality to master as it is most people's first impulse to make friends with the people they work with. This will ultimately lead to disaster however as there will always come a time when the leader must be a leader and not a friend. Cut this inevitable paradox off at the pass, treat your team well but make sure it is clear where your loyalties lie.

Be decisive: Being a leader means making the sorts of decisions that other folks don't want to make. Being the sort of leader that separates themselves from the crowd means accepting this fact and seeing every decision you make through to the end. This doesn't mean to make all decisions in a vacuum; however, a good leader knows when it is time to gather input and when it is time to act. A leader who is known to be decisive will be supported by their team when they must make quick decisions as they will have a history of quality decisions to back them up.

Be empathetic: One part of being a leader than many people struggle with is giving criticism when it is due. Having empathy for the people you are responsible for does not mean avoiding criticism or always giving in to their requests; rather, it means taking their feelings into account and dealing with issues appropriately.

Help your team to grow as individuals: Your team is only as strong as its weakest member which is why it is important to encourage your team to grow under your leadership. You can ensure this is the case by taking the time to get to know each member of your team and their specific strengths and weaknesses. Take the time to provide them with leadership opportunities of their own and to find ways to help them shine while improving the team at the same time. Everyone has something unique to offer the group, a good leader can determine what that is and help nourish it for the good of the whole.

Follow your own example: If you want your team to arrive early, work late, always be prepared and work as hard as possible you need to be willing to go the extra mile with them. A leader who preaches hard work and sacrifice but commits to neither is not the sort of leader that a team will follow for any reasonable period. Sometimes being the leader means towing a difficult party line thrown down by someone higher in the chain of command, your team will take difficult changes much better if they know you are with them in practice and not just in spirit.

This goes for positive changes as well as negative ones. Your team will follow your lead, if you want to have a more open collaborative workspace, get your team involved. If you want them to take more initiative, make the decision to let them make their own decisions. Do as I say and not as I do may work when dealing with children, but your team will spot any hypocrisy and It will poison your relationship with them permanently. Stick to uniformity when it comes to which rules apply to whom and you will be much happier in the long run.

Consider Your Body Language

Show them you are the leader: It is important that you try to project as strong and powerful of body language cues as possible when around your team to help you appear to be as full of leadership material as possible. This will help you seem more trustworthy as well as more competent, two things that are especially important for a new leader to possess. Even better, acting this way will help you feel both more in control of the situation which will make you better equipped to handle the task you have been given. It is important to not be so authoritative that you lose the ability to speak with your team in a tacit fashion.

Be aware of your stature: Having the right stature is about more than standing the right way and stopping yourself from slouching, though this is extremely important as well. A good leader is never tired and always willing to go the extra mile for their team. If you want to have the stature of a leader you are going to want to modify your nonverbal cues to ensure you project the types of cues, you expect a leader to project whenever you are with your team. This doesn't mean that you always must have all the answer and a clear grasp of what is coming next, it just means your team needs to feel that they are being led in a competent fashion.

Don't get to close: A good leader has the respect of their team, but always remains apart from them as well. This means you need to give off the nonverbal cues to ensure they know they can talk to you but keep enough of a distance that they don't feel as though they can question you when things get rough. It can be a difficult line to walk but it is crucial to do so if you hope to be an effective leader.

Watch for barriers: Other important body languages to be on the lookout for includes anything that generates a physical barrier. Common examples of this are crossed arms or holding documents or other props in hand and pressed tightly to the chest. These are all signs that the other person is not receptive to what the other person is saying. In fact, one study looked at more than 2,000 negotiations take place and none of them ended in success if one member never uncrossed their arms.

These behaviors show that the person in question is either emotionally or mentally blocked off from whatever is going on in front of them. This is an unintentional habit which is what makes it so useful when it comes to getting to the heart of the matter. Likewise, if a person starts off using this type of body language, and then changes their tune, you will know that you have managed to win them over to your side.

Copycat: When discussing something important with another person, the easiest way to tell if you are winning them over to your side is if you catch them copying your body language. It could be something as simple as a hand gesture or crossing or uncrossing your legs, the specific action doesn't matter all that matters is that it happened at all. If the other person starts mimicking the things you do, then you know that whatever argument you are using is working.

An interesting fact is that this type of copycat behavior is not only indicative of what the other person is currently thinking, it can also influence opinions as well. As such, if you can get the other person to start copying your movements, you can make it more likely that they are going to start agreeing with you as well. In order to set up this type of scenario, you will want to start by subtly copying the things the other person does.

Fake it: Specifically, you may find that faking a degree of confidence in your leadership skills that you don't yet feel can be an extremely effective way to improve social interactions of all types, without having to have fully deal with the issues that may be at the root of your lack of confidence. While this might sound ridiculous, take a moment and consider a scenario where you were interacting with a person who you identify as being supremely confident. Now consider all the things about this person that made you believe they were confident and ask yourself how would you have known if they were faking it?

The truth of the matter is that if you act confidently in each situation then those around you will have no reason to assume you feel otherwise. As such, pretending to have confidence and being confident are two sides of the same coin. What's more, having success when pretending to have confidence once, will make it much easier to do a second time, and what's more, each additional time you pretend to have confidence you will have to pretend less and less until you won't be pretending at all.

In order to act the way a confident person would act in each situation; all you need to do is to visualize someone you know who is confident and then ask yourself what they would do if they were in your position. From there, it is just a matter of following their lead. Think about the way they would present themselves, what type of gestures they would use, what type of body language they would utilize and how they would speak. With a good role model to follow you will be surprised at how easy playing pretend can be.

Incremental improvement: One of the major duties of an effective leader is to constantly evaluate different aspects of the team in order to ensure it is operating at peak efficiency. The leader will also need to keep up to date on customer requirements as this is something that is going to be constantly changing as well. Doing so is one of the only truly reliable ways of staying ahead of the curve by making it possible to streamline the overall direction of the team towards the processes that will achieve the best results.

In order to ensure that this is the case, an effective leader will want to make time in their schedule to look at the results and then compare them to the costs as a means of discovering the best ways to use all the resources available to them at the given time. This will include things like evaluating the organization in hopes of making it more efficient and reliable.

Chapter 7:
Improve Your Emotional Intelligence

Emotional Intelligence (or, EQ) is "the ability to identify and manage your own emotions and the emotions of others." This includes three skills:

- Emotional awareness

- The ability to harness and apply emotions to tasks

- The ability to manage emotions

While it may seem like a simple concept, the truth is not many people are very high in Emotional Intelligence. How would someone even know if they were Emotionally Intelligent and, more importantly, how it might be affecting their life?

There are so many theories on Emotional Intelligence, why it's important and how it can be used. However, there are a few key elements to EQ that seem to be found in every discussion. The first, and arguably most important, element is self-awareness since without knowing and understanding yourself, your own emotions, your triggers, etc., how can you perform any self-assessment to grow or improve? Correctly identifying your own emotions is the basis for EQ.

Self-regulation comes from self-awareness. Once you are in sync with your own emotions and understand when and why you feel them, you can then regulate them. In other words, if you know that you get very angry when someone talks down to you, you can prepare yourself to preemptively disrupt your anger.

Thinking before acting is key in controlling emotions as well as withholding judgement of others. Most people tend to react in emotionally intense situations, having angry outbursts when something goes wrong or taking constructive criticism personally to the point of becoming depressed. People also tend to judge others before trying to understand why that person is saying, doing or feeling something. Self-regulation allows you to put yourself in another's shoes which allows for a positive emotional response as opposed to a careless reaction.

EQ Is Not for The Lazy.

When it comes to your day to day interactions with others, empathy is hands-down one of the most valuable elements of emotional intelligence. While it is often confused with either compassion or sympathy, empathy is the ability to understand and relate to the emotions of another person. It directly relates back to withholding judgement, which is reinforced through self-regulation. Those who have a high degree of empathy can understand when others are feeling a specific way and respond according to their goals and desires.

For example, if someone is depressed because they didn't get a promotion, the empath will try to cheer that person up and redirect them from the depressed state even if they don't much care one way or the other. Empathy is the difference between listening to what someone is saying and understanding what they are feeling.

Those with naturally high EQ are often leaders because they have a natural ability to connect with others, manage their emotions and inspire them in one way or another. This is often a natural result of the other elements of emotional intelligence and it is possible the leader in question isn't even doing such things intentionally, their situation is just a result of their innate abilities.

Getting Started

If you feel as though your EQ may not be where you want it to be, there are several simple exercises you can start with to help you move in the right direction. You are going to want to practice the following at least twice a day, once in the morning and once at night to keep you in an emotionally intelligent mindset. When choosing the time to start your exercises, ensure that it is a time you can easily repeat each day as your mind will take to the practice more easily with the added repetition. Finally, you will want to practice each day for a full month in order to ensure these exercises become full-blown habits.

Practice Active Listening: During arguments or disagreements, we often listen not to understand but to react and respond. When the other person is speaking, we are almost mentally constructing out own arguments to answer back or give back to them. This leads to even more conflict.

Dealing with conflict becomes more effective when you tackle issues in an assertive yet respective manner, without being defensive. When you listen empathetically, your own thoughts and emotions are considered. Listening actively and empathetically can help you shed toxic feelings building up in you.

Be assertive, but also practice active listening to find that one point that can lead to a resolution. Problem solution only happens when you understand where the other person is coming from and what they want. You can find a middle ground only when you tune in to the words, feelings, and emotions of the other person, not just to give a fitting reply but also to resolve the issue. Listening is all about putting the other person's words, thoughts, and feelings first.

Your opinion about people or events may not change. However, the time spent listening to the other person may just calm you and help you come up with a more positive or constructive response. It may help you see things from a different perspective and analyze the situation more objectively.

Practice being more lighthearted: When you are more lighthearted and optimistic, it is simpler to capture the goodness of everyday situations and objects. Positivity results in greater emotional happiness and increased opportunities. People are forever looking to be around optimistic folks who come up with positive connections and possibilities. When you become more negative, you only concentrate on what can go awry rather than building strong resistance.

People with a more evolved emotional quotient know how to utilize wit and humor to make everyone feel happier, positive and safer. They know the art of using laugher to tide over tough times.

Learn to take note of how you are feeling: For most people, each day is a jumble of appointments and deadlines that make it difficult to find an extra moment to breathe, much less take stock of their emotional state. Unfortunately, getting into this mindset will make it much easier for actions to slip through subconsciously that are a response to the emotional state in question. Therefore, it is important to practice communicating with yourself and prioritize those communications when they do occur.

Emotions are often tied to events that are currently taking place in your immediate surroundings, but unfortunately, that doesn't mean the emotion is a valid response to the events. The emotion might instead be tied to a previous event that the current situation is simply recalling. If this is the case, while the emotion might feel totally real to you, it is in no way relevant to the scenario in question. Learning to understand which emotions you are feeling and why is an important step towards improving your EQ.

Being aware of your feelings is a skill which means that like any other skill it will only improve with practice. As such, it is important to pick a specific time every morning and every evening where you can check-in on your feelings and determine the root cause of whatever you find. This should be a pair of relatively busy points so that the odds of you experiencing a relatively complex emotion is somewhat high for the best effect. Consider the physical response the emotion is eliciting and how it makes you feel and make sure you connect it to a specific emotion and find that emotion's source.

Figure out what triggers the emotion. Everyone has a trigger when it comes to their emotions. It is not random when you get mad and explode at the people around you. If you want to start working on your emotional intelligence and get it to work for you, it is important that you learn what some of these triggers are all about.

For many people, the triggers that come with anger would include something that stress or insecurities. When they are dealing with a lot of stress at work or home or elsewhere, they are more likely to lash out at even the smallest thing. But is it worth harming other people and making them feel bad because you are a little bit stressed out about something? Learning how to properly manage your stress levels and keep them low is one of the best things that you can do in this situation.

If it is your insecurities that are causing issues, you may need to work on whatever is causing that in your life. Just because someone says something or constructively critiques you at work doesn't mean that you can just blow up and act in a violent or horrible way. Learning how to deal with these insecurities, or even what is causing those insecurities, can make a big difference in how you will react to others.

There are many triggers that can cause you to act out when your emotions are started. But you must be the one who is in control of those emotions, no matter what. Learning what those triggers are and taking care of them as quickly as possible will ensure that you will be able to control your emotions instead of letting them take over your life.

Own up to your actions: Accepting complete responsibility for your actions is one of the first steps towards developing higher emotional quotient. People who are emotionally intelligent don't feel the need to shift responsibility on someone else, justify their wrongdoings or defend themselves aggressively. They shy away from putting the blame elsewhere and completely own up to the mistake.

On the contrary, they accept responsibility for their actions and learn important lessons from it. Unlike people low on emotional intelligence or self-esteem, they do not ascribe their mistakes to external circumstances or factors that are supposedly outside their control. They accept their choices, bad decisions and less than perfect actions.

When you accept your mistakes, it is easier to control, be responsible for and manage your feelings and behavior in the future. Blaming the situation or another person only takes away from helping you control the situation more effectively moving ahead. It also helps you gain a perspective about your own abilities and weaknesses. When acknowledging that something went wrong as a result of your choices and decisions, you are in a more gainful position to tackle it.

You acquire the ability to control your emotions, manage negative feelings, develop more fruitful interpersonal relationships, wield better decisions and influencer your actions more positively. You are not replying on others or external circumstances for determining your emotions but taking charge of how you feel.

Tap into your inner passions: Everyone goes about their daily routine and work in a mechanical manner. However, there's always something that excites you or triggers your passion? What is it that you're most upbeat about doing? To move out of the rut, and gain more emotional stability or greater peace, take up a pursuit you are passionate about. This will lower your stress levels, release feel good chemicals in the brain, and increase your ability to handle emotions more effectively. When you are less stressed, it is easier to be in control of your feelings.

Manage your stress and anxiety: Stress and anxiety are your worst friends when you are trying to get a handle on your emotions. They will leave you feeling on edge and it won't take much for someone to push you over. Our modern day lives have made it easy to feel stressed out on a regular basis. From work to school to taking care of kids and more, it is a miracle that any of us can keep up with it

Stephen Patterson

all. Luckily, there are a lot of great options that you can choose from to help relieve the stress and make yourself feel better.

There are so many ways that you can work on your own stress and anxiety and the method that you use may include one of the other options that we have discussed in this guidebook. For example, a lot of people like to journal out their feelings and frustrations, and this can be a great way to increase your self-awareness as well. You may decide to go out on a walk to help reduce the impact of your emotions, so you don't react right away. Some people like to pick up a hobby, talk out their emotions with a friend, take a relaxing bath, or do something else that helps them get rid of the stress and feel so much better.

Picking out a method that helps you manage your stress and anxiety is so important. If you are feeling stressed and anxious all the time, it is going to be hard for you to concentrate on keeping those emotions in check. Find the stress reliever that works for you and make sure to keep it on hand whenever you may need it.

Chapter 8:
Improve Your Ability to Remain in Control

When it comes to remaining in control of your situation no matter what, the first thing you need to understand is that there is a difference between being in control and never being spontaneous. Instead, those who are truly in control always can remain aware of their situation and their personal state so that they can course correct at any point things stop going according to plan. Learning to be in control always means understanding your strengths and weakness as well as what can be done in any given situation to maximize the one while minimizing the other. Learning to take control of any situation will help you to master your emotions and ultimately live the type of life you have always dreamed of.

Controlling the current situation: If you find yourself in a situation that is rapidly spiraling out of control, the first thing you are going to want to do is to take a moment to calm yourself. If you are too distraught over whatever it is that is currently going on, then you will find it much more difficult to think clearly and critically about the situation you find yourself in. You may find that the breathing and relaxation exercises discussed in Chapter 5 are a big help when it comes to quickly and effectively calming yourself now.

With this out of the way, the next thing to do is to take stock of what you need to do first in order to start getting the situation under control. While it is important to plan, if possible, there is a chance you will need to take care of the most pressing issues first before taking the time to consider what the best course of action might be moving forward. When you do find the time to start planning it is important to ensure that you don't let your emotions or insignificant details distract you from what matters most.

If you are dealing with the current situation alone, you will find that sketching out a general plan of attack will help to immediately make you feel as though you are more in control of the current situation and thus ready to face whatever might be coming next. If you are with a group, the first person who can assess the situation and put together a plan that makes sense is likely going to be the one that everyone else falls in line behind.

When it comes to creating a plan in the moment, it is important to understand that you don't need to have absolutely all the details worked out beforehand, as long as you take the details you do have and work out the most logical course of action based on the specifics of those details. When looking to take control of a situation in the moment, if you wait until you have all the relevant details before you make a move then you risk being too late to the party and either not being able to do anything meaningful to move the situation towards your desired resolution or having to follow someone else's lead while they take charge instead.

Additionally, you may find that you have more confidence moving forward if you take a second to consider what variables you can control in the current situation. For example, if you are planning an event that will be taking place outdoors then it is impossible to control the weather but if it starts raining in the moment then you can do what you can to change the location or look for a means of keeping the current location dry.

When you are first getting used to taking charge in these types of situations, it is only natural to feel hesitant before speaking up, especially if this will lead to you overseeing a group of relative strangers. Therefore, it is important to take the immediate reaction that is required without hesitation so that you can do the right thing without worrying about getting waylaid by thoughts of doubt. While this will no doubt seem like a harrowing proposition at first, once you have leapt into action a few times you will find that the thought of doing so becomes far more manageable.

Stephen Patterson

If you find yourself the person most prepared to lead others in an urgent situation then it is important that you speak in a commanding tone that expresses the fact that you have things under control. When it comes to explaining your plan to a group it is important that you don't push to get your own way and instead let the others decide what to do with the path you have provided them. Not forcing the issues shows that you are confident in the details you have set forth and means that anyone who doesn't like what you have to say will have to come up with a superior alternative.

An important part of taking charge of a given situation in the moment is the effective delegation of duties. Making sure that everyone has a part to play that suits their abilities requires not only an understanding of the situation, but an ability to understand what the strengths and weaknesses of others are. This goes for yourself as well, if you know that your leadership skills are not up to the task then there is no harm in putting forth your plan and then delegating the role of carrying it out to someone else. Getting through an urgent situation successfully means putting your personal feelings aside and doing what needs to be done in order to ensure success.

Controlling internal situations: When it comes to controlling any type of emotional turmoil you might be feeling, the first thing you will want to keep in mind is that it is important to not bottle up your emotions and instead to always really feel whatever it is that you are feeling. Welcoming your emotions and accepting them is the only way to truly understand them and thus control them effectively. Repressing your emotions doesn't mean you are in control it means you are letting them control you. suppressing your feelings in the long-term can lead to a wide variety of health problems including things like chronic pain, insomnia, and even heart disease.

The first thing you are going to want to do when it comes to ensuring you can properly control your emotions is always to keep a small journal with you that you can log your feelings in. This will make it easier for you to find out what is leading up to each outburst of feeling as well as your response to the emotion and how that response made you feel after the fact. This should make it possible for you to keep track of your triggers for various emotions, which is the first step to limiting them in a meaningful way.

You may also find it helpful if you take the extra step of giving your own painful memories that just won't leave you alone, longstanding insecurities or any other reoccurring bad thoughts you have your own unique name. For example, if you find yourself getting angry when someone cuts you off in traffic, not just annoyed but bordering on physical violence, then simply owing it as road rage can be surprisingly effective. The fact of the matter is that names have power, not only will naming these types of thoughts and feelings makes it easier for you to pinpoint when they are causing you to act irrationally, it will also give you some control over it as well.

Giving something a name is important because it also gives whatever is being named clear definition and context. Without a name, the feeling is just something nebulous that takes control when and where it wants to. Once it has a name it can be prepared against and ultimately controlled. When you feel the named feeling or thought coming on you can greet it by name and prepare yourself for what's coming next which should help you get some distance on things overall, thus preventing the negative thought or feeling from taking hold.

If you find that you lose control when certain thoughts or memories occur to you then this is likely because you are holding onto longstanding resentment, grudges, and anger. Making a conscious effort to forgive those who have betrayed you and feel compassion for those that have harmed you will not only make it easier to deal with any related thoughts or memories, it will also make you more resilient in the future because you have learned to keep your negative feelings under control.

Finally, if you find that your emotions are still more in control than you might like, then you might find talking to a professional to be a useful way to right whatever issues might be overtaking you. You may find that regularly talking to someone can help you come to terms with the patterns you fall into most often and, more importantly, learn new and improved responses to ensure you don't keep making the same mistakes time and again.

Take control in the long-term. Even if you can take control of a situation in the moment, you may still find it difficult to get things together enough to properly plan for the future. If this is the case, then you may find that simply taking stock of your issues will help you get back on track. It doesn't matter what issues you are dealing with, if you write them all down in order of importance then by the end you are sure to see that many are more manageable than you first expected.

If you find that you are having trouble getting started, then you are likely putting up too many mental filters. To get past them all you need to do is to set a timer for five minutes and then write down anything and everything that comes to mind until the timer goes off. While many of the things that you write likely won't make the cut upon closer consideration, you will almost surely come up with enough useful material to move forward with.

When making your list it is important to be as specific as possible and to also be honest with yourself as the only person you will hurt by lying is yourself. If you find that you still can't get past your mental filters, then you may want to get an outside perspective instead. You could try asking a friend or loved one for their opinions and use their observations to get your own creative juices flowing.

Once you have a good list to work from, the next step towards controlling your future is to set goals that will make your list come true. The specifics of setting appropriate goals is discussed in detail in chapter 12. Once you have your goals in mind, in order to ensure you control the outcome as much as possible it is important to utilize a technique known as mental contrasting. Mental contrasting involves looking at a specific task and then considering all the potential obstacles that could potentially get in the way of its completion. All you need to do is to take a few minutes to think about what could go wrong and what you can do in order to ensure that this is not the case.

When it comes to dealing with tasks that involve other people it is important to set clear boundaries as to what is and is not acceptable and then stick to them. Likewise, it is important to respect boundaries that others set. It doesn't matter how healthy the relationship is, it should still have boundaries. It is also important to remain on the lookout for emotional manipulation as this can easily derail an otherwise promising plan in unexpected ways.

Mental Toughness Mindset

In addition to taking care of your mental health, it is important to take care of your physical health as well. This includes things like getting enough sleep each night and eating right. Remember, if you aren't taking the time to properly take control of your physical, mental, and emotional health then you can't always be in control.

Chapter 9:
Improve Your Ability to Trust Your Instincts

Conventional wisdom points out the importance of trusting one's gut but then gives very little guidance as to how to go about doing so. This type of gut instinct, also known as intuition, has to do with a person's innate understanding of a situation. It doesn't require additional research or follow up; it is just something you know. Intuition often arises as a type of feeling in the body that is unique to each person but odds are you have felt it from time to time when you knew deep down in your bones that, whatever you were doing at the time, you were on the right track.

Learning to listen to what your intuition has to say can make it easier to avoid potentially dangerous situations or potentially unhealthy relationships. Throughout your life, you will find many people have plans and ideas about your future, some with your best interests in mind and others not so much. It can often be difficult to tell what category a specific person falls into, but if you put aside all those external thoughts and opinions and list to your intuition instead then it is more likely to point you in the right direction.

Unfortunately, trusting your gut isn't something you can simply make the decision to do, it is a skill which means that much like any other skill it will only improve with practice. Luckily, even if you have never relied on your intuition before, it is still a part of you which means you can still reach it if you try. The following tips will help you start to draw it out more regularly in your day to day life.

Consider the things that get in the way: Your intuition acts much like the North Start which means that, if you aren't vigilant, things can get in the way of it telling you where to go next. Once you become aware of these obstructions, however, you'll find that it becomes much easier to tell when you are heading towards them and course correct accordingly.

One of the most common obstructions is overthinking which is the opposite of letting intuition guide you. Intuition is all about instinct, and if you spend too much time thinking and not enough time acting them you will find that you can't tune in to whatever it is your intuition is trying to get you to do. While planning is an important part of being successful in many instances, putting too much thought into a decision can make it difficult to ever actually get anything done.

If you find yourself stuck in this type of situation then it is likely that your thought process is being blocked or is working hard to build a case for the opposite decision compared to the one you just made up your mind about. This is known as analysis paralysis and it occurs when there are too many possible variables to make the process of making a choice manageable.

Another consequence of overthinking is an influx of considerations outlining why a specific course of action should have been taken as opposed to the one you decided on or why a course of action you are considering is almost guaranteed to go wrong. In these types of situations, you will often find that you are basing your presumed behavior based on what others expect, prefer, or think, as opposed to how you feel in the moment. This type of "should" thinking shifts the focus from internal to external, thus decreasing your ability to access your intuition.

Even though both unconscious biases and prejudices are essentially the opposite of overthinking a given scenario, they still have the same overall effect on your intuition. These sorts of biases serve to cause you to operate based on quick judgements that the brain automatically spits out based on what it believes it has learned from past experiences, regardless of whether these past experiences are true. As a result, they bypass any type of rational thought, making it impossible for you to tap into your intuition to determine the true course of action.

Accept your intuition: Another reason that many people have a hard time utilizing their intuition to its full effect is that accepting your intuition means listening to what it has to tell you, even when what it has to tell you isn't what you want to hear. Likewise, as it isn't a physical, or well-defined, sensation, it can be easy to brush it off, especially when it is telling you to do something that goes contrary to your regular nature.

For example, if you usually take a shortcut home from the bus stop through an alley but feel a tug in the back of your mind saying you should find another way home, you may want to ignore that fear as taking the long way around would add 20 minutes to your walk and you are tired after a long day. If you know enough to trust your intuition, however, then you would nevertheless make the trade off and find yourself feeling better about the trip almost immediately. Before you can trust your gut for good, however, you need to welcome intuition into your life, even if it doesn't always make sense, while at the same time making a commitment to it that you will follow where it leads.

Grow your intuition in the right way: After you have opened yourself up to the idea of being more receptive to your intuition, the next thing you will need to work on is experiencing it to the fullest. To do so successfully, you are going to want to find a quiet place where you can tune out the stress and distractions of your daily life. If you are rarely all by yourself then you may want to prepare yourself mentally for the change as it can be pretty jarring as you will be faced with all sides of yourself in a way that can be a bit intense for some people.

You may find that hidden emotions emerge from your mental depths and that you have issues to resolve that you previously weren't aware of. This is nothing to worry about, however, and is, indeed, all part of the process. This is also a key step as when you are truly alone you won't have anyone telling you what to do or what to think, you will be able to listen to yourself and see what your intuition has to say.

This will also allow you to clear your mind and slow down which can make it easier to break free of the haze most people find themselves in most of the time. It doesn't matter if you are physically or mentally tired, either way, it means you end up being at less than your best which makes it easier to miss information your intuition has been trying to tell you. Slowing own will also help you to better process and recognize the information you do receive in your mind and body.

This means you must push away the physical and mental clutter surrounding you by doing what you can in order to remove the greatest sense of urgency from the situation whether this is pushing back an upcoming deadline or physically stepping away from the situation either mentally or physically until you are free to finally listen to whatever it is that your intuition has been trying to tell you.

On the other hand, slowing down means taking deliberate actions to find space for your intuition to occupy. Sticking with a slower pace makes it easier to shift your perspective and clear away excess distractions so that you can feel and see the things that your intuition says matter the most. If you find it hard to physically get away from the issues that you are dealing with then mindfulness meditation, discussed in detail in the next chapter, could help as well.

Focus on yourself: Focusing on yourself can be as simple as looking inward to determine what you need to do in order to be successful in the current situation. This is a rare time where it is perfectly fine to make everything all about you which means you may need to give yourself permission to do so beforehand. If you find yourself shifting back to focusing on the wants and needs of others make a concentrated effort to return your focus back to being curious about your personal wants and needs which is how you will most reliably activate your intuition as concentrating on your specific needs helps clear the way to a direct connection.

Stephen Patterson

Becoming aware of your intuition and acting on it are two very different things, however, which means that while you are first learning to trust your gut it is important that you also learn to observe when your intuition starts to pop up in a given situation. For example, if you are looking for a new job and come across one that fits your criteria in every way imaginable on paper, but doesn't feel quite right in practice, what would you do? If you are like most people you would turn down the job no matter what the benefits looked like, simply because something inside of you says it doesn't feel right.

In order to strengthen this feeling, you may want to write everything down in an intuition journal that will make it easier for you to notice future instances of your intuition doing its thing because you will be able to compare them to previous instances where something similar occurred. You will want to keep this journal close by and write down all your relevant experiences for at least a month until you are able to discern clear patterns. This will help you to get to know yourself more thoroughly and understand just how often intuition plays a role in your life.

Acting: Once you have gotten used to listening for your intuition, the next thing you are going to need to do is use it to make positive changes to your actions which can be easier said than done. As it is not always clear what you need to do for your intuition to give you the all-clear. As such, when you are first getting started it doesn't matter what steps you take, if you get in the habit of taking them on the regular. These small steps can help you learn that listening to your intuition is beneficial until you eventually reach a point where listening to your intuition and reacting to it are essentially one in the same.

Chapter 10:
Improve Your Mental Fortitude

Since its inception, mindfulness meditation been proven via scientific study to improve the physical wellbeing of those that practice it on a regular basis. At its heart, mindfulness meditation is all about focusing your mind to ensure that you are as fully aware of each moment as fully as possible. This, in turn, allows you to exist more completely in any given moment by expanding your consciousness to the fullest.

While it might sound like a tall order at first, the truth of the matter is that being mindful is a skill which means it can be improved by regular practice in much the same way as any other skill. Luckily, practicing mindfulness meditation is as easy as finding a few moments to focus solely on the present and the information that your senses are providing you now. In fact, if you can find just fifteen minutes a day to practice, you will soon find that your overall stress is likely to decrease, and your sense of self is likely to be at an all-time high. This isn't just an ephemeral feeling either, neuroimaging performed on those who practice mindfulness meditation on a regular basis shows that their minds actually process information more effectively, they are able to more easily regulate their emotions and their attention spans than those who do not make the practice a part of their daily routine.

Furthermore, the sooner you begin practicing mindfulness meditation, the greater the chance that doing so will ensure your brain retains more volume as you age, dramatically improving overall brain health as a result. This increased vitality also reaches the hippocampus which, in turn, makes it easier to learn and retain new information with minimal effort. At the same time, the amygdala becomes less active which means that the amount of fear, stress, and anxiety that you experience will be decreased as well.

Beyond the physical changes, regularly practicing mindfulness has been shown to decrease instances of participant's minds getting stuck in negative thought patterns while at the same time increasing focus. This should not come as a surprise given the fact that a recent Johns Hopkins study found that regularly practicing mindfulness meditation is equally effective at treating depression, ADD and anxiety. It also improves verbal reasoning skills as shown in a study which found that GRE students who practiced mindfulness performed up to 16 points better than their peers.

Bonus Benefits

- Practicing mindfulness has been shown to lower stress by decreasing the amount of the hormone cortisol the body produces.

- Practicing mindfulness can provide you with the opportunity to know the inner you and reveal ways to make yourself even better.

- Practicing mindfulness will help improve your ability to retain facts in both the short and long term.

- Practicing mindfulness will help keep you healthy. Those who regularly practice mindfulness meditation tend to report fewer sick days and that they recover from illnesses faster.

- Practicing mindfulness has been shown to improve the practitioner's ability to control their emotions and enhance their tolerance for pain.

- Practicing mindfulness can make music sound better. Those who meditate regularly often report an ability to more fully engage with music they hear and seem to enjoy it more.

- Practicing mindfulness will make you more empathetic towards others. Mindfulness meditation has been shown to make practitioners less judgmental, more compassionate and more active listeners.

Getting Started

While one of the best things about mindfulness meditation is its malleable nature, when you are first getting started it is recommended that you set some time aside each day to specifically devote to the practice. Ideally, this should be someplace that is quiet and during a period when you feel relaxed and where you can devote as much as thirty minutes to going deep within yourself without fear of worldly distractions. Remember, being mindful is all about creating space between the sensory information that your body is always sending to your mind and your reactions to that information so the fewer stimuli you have to deal with at the start, the easier you will find the practice to be.

Choose a set time and stick to it: As with any burgeoning habit, it is important that you create a routine for your mindfulness meditation and stay with it if you hope for the practice to stick. It typically takes 30 days for a new habit to take root in your daily schedule which is why it is important to commit fully to practicing mindfulness meditation if you ever want it to become part of your routine. Due to its low impact nature, nothing external is required, it is very easy for many people to make excuses to get out of meditating, especially if their daily schedule is already filled to bursting.

If you find yourself always coming up with an excuse to get out of meditating now, you may find the following piece of advice particularly useful. "Practice mindfulness meditation for fifteen minutes every day unless, of course, you are extremely busy in which case you should practice for thirty minutes instead." Don't let the outside world intrude on your potential for inner peace, find a time each day that works for you and stick with it no matter what; in a month's time, you will be glad you did.

Focus on the moment: While your end goal, while being mindful, should be to find a state of internal calm, regardless of what is going on in the world around you, it is difficult for most people to reach this state right away. Rather, they find it easier to start quieting their thoughts by focusing all their attention on the signals that their bodies are relaying to them now.

While, at first, you may not feel as though you are processing too much data from the world around you, especially if you are practicing in a quiet, calm space as suggested, this could not be further from the truth. The fact of the matter is that most of the time your brain filters out around 80 percent of the information it receives on a given day which means that information is there, you just need to get in the habit of accessing it regularly.

Over time, you will learn to tune out the thoughts you have regarding your everyday routines and instead tap directly into whatever it is that is going on around you. When you do so, it is important to process the information that your senses are providing you, while at the same time making a conscious effort to not pass judgement or dig too deeply into anything that crosses your mind. Judging results in additional thoughts, one way or another, which tend to lead to even more thoughts, until it is practically impossible for you to focus on the task at hand.

Remember, when it comes to mindfulness meditation, the goal is to get as close as you can manage to the moment as possible, which means ignoring everything else that is going on, except for what your senses are providing you. To reach this state, you will start by focusing on your breathing, especially on the way the air feels as it enters and exits your lungs, along with the way it smells and tastes.

Extend your senses outward, beyond your body to the room around you. Listen deeply and pick up the small sounds of the world around you that you are typically too busy to really hear. Notice the silence as well, just as important as the noise for its counterpoint. As with the thoughts you are keeping at bay, it is important to not do anything more with the sounds than simply accept them as they are. Don't pass judgement, don't use them to make assumptions about what is making them; simply let them wash over you and hear them in their purity.

From sounds, you should then move on to smells, strive to smell beyond the dominate smells in the room and pick up the fainter, more ingrained smells that you typically miss. Once more, the depth of the interaction should stop at registering the smell, proceed any farther down the path of interaction and you are no longer really in the moment. Acceptance of the stimuli you are receiving and cooperation with the universe at large should be your goal now, but this is no time to think about that.

Finally, bring the exercise back to a more internal point by considering any tastes that might be currently in your mouth. This is another instance that will require you to mentally turn off the filters that automatically diminish all sensation to the point of being manageable, don't let yourself accept that your mouth is currently barren, go deeper and find the taste that is truly there.

Once you cannot hold your focus any longer, gradually lose your control of the moment and let the world at large back in slowly, so as not to add too much stress back in too soon. Remember how you felt during the mediation, however, and strive to recreate that feeling in the world at large.

Extra Tips

Be consistent: This is probably the most difficult part of meditation. Without time, we find it easy to make an excuse to skip meditating for the day. Don't. Meditation doesn't require leaving your home or any kind of special equipment. All you need is your time and some space.

Observe the moment: Mindfulness is not necessarily quieting the mind or finding an eternal state of calmness. The goal here is simple. You want to pay attention to the moment you are in without judging. When you judge a thought or something you have done in the past, you tend to dwell on it. That isn't living in the moment and is not conducive to mindful meditation. While this is easier said than done, it is a crucial step to mindful meditation. With practice, it will be easy to achieve. Be mindful of the moment, of your senses and your surroundings.

Always come back to observation and the present moment. It is easy for our minds to get lost in thought. Mindfulness meditation is the art of bringing yourself back to the moment, over and over, as many times as it takes. Don't get discouraged. In the beginning, you will find your mind wanders a lot. Reel it back in and keep moving forward.

Be kind: Even if your mind does happen to wander, and it will don't be hard on yourself. It happens. Acknowledge whatever thoughts pop up, put them to the side and get back on track.

As you can see, the basics are quite simple. These are the things you need to remember daily while you are practicing. What's important is that you find the time to implement the basics every day. Mastering the basics will make it much simpler for you to dive into the deeper aspects of mindful meditation, which we will be discussing a little later.

Practice mindfulness during your Commute: Ensuring that you remain mindful during your commute will help you focus on the day ahead in such a way that you are sure to reach your destination calm, focused and ready to make the most of the time ahead. As being mindful is akin to being extremely present in each moment it will also ensure you are driving as safely as possible. By training your brain to stay in the present instead of thinking about the past or worrying about the future you, in turn, allow it to focus a substantial portion of energy on making the most of the now and getting the most from each work day.

Start as soon as you get into your vehicle by vocalizing your intention to be mindful during your morning commute. Then take a few deep breaths and use this time to become more aware of your body. Become aware of your hands on the steering wheel and what they feel beneath them. Become aware of your body and the sensations it feels as it is pressed against your seat. Feel your foot on the pedal and the resistance it feels as you prepare to drive. As you begin your drive take in the world around you while at the same time striving to be aware of the act of seeing, of the act of hearing. Try to focus on these three things, body, sights, sounds and only these things for the length of your drive.

That's really all there is to it, though like many things it is much easier said than done. Today's society is obsessed with multi-tasking and as such your mind will want to wander, thoughts will try and sneak their way in, you will want to think about the things waiting for you at work or tasks you left unfinished at home. Your phone will make at least one noise and you will be tempted to see the specifics of the notification. It is important to ignore these obstacles.

Stephen Patterson

Chapter 11:
Improve Your Assertiveness

When it comes to learning to be assertive, everyone is going to come to the task with a different mindset and different expectations as to what the result will be. As such, the first step to becoming a more assertive individual is understanding just what assertiveness is and what it is not.

Unfortunately, what is and what is not assertive behavior is often muddled by the fact that, if you aren't careful, you can easily overstep the line and end up being aggressive rather than assertive. A person who is assertive when it comes to their needs is admired, a person who is aggressive for these same things is seen as a menace. Despite the serious differences between the two, it is still easy to confuse them, especially for those who are still learning about the finer points of assertiveness. As such, a definition of the two is useful in telling one from the other.

Assertiveness: At its heart, assertiveness is all about balance. It requires that you be in tune with yourself in order to accurately determine your wants and needs beforehand so that you can compare them to the wants and needs of those you meet. Those who are assertive are self-assured and confident and use that inner strength to get their point across in a way that be both fair and empathetic to the other person's point of view.

Aggressiveness: Aggressive behavior, on the other hand, is completely based around winning. Those who are aggressive rather than assertive are going to do what is in their own best interest without any thought for the desires, feelings, needs, and rights of others. Those who are aggressive use the personal power they might have for selfish gains and are often seen as bullying or pushy by others. They take what they want, when they want it and damn the consequences.

Focus on I statements: Statements that include sentiments such as "I want" or "I feel" make it easier for you to get your point across in a way that is both effective and clear. Additionally, the use of the word "I" should serve to let the other party know that perception is relative and what you are saying doesn't diminish whatever they are thinking or feeling. Furthermore, you will find that it helps you to keep the facts separate from whatever it is you want out of the scenario instead to help ensure you get the best possible outcome each time.

Escalate properly: If you find that your first attempt at being assertive fails, then you may need to consider escalating your approach significantly if you wish to get your point across. This will include things like taking a firm, yet respectful, tone while still working to be polite. This is not the same as increasing the emotional intensity of the conversation as this will just make you seem aggressive, put the other person on the defensive, and ultimately do little to solve whatever the real problem of the moment might be. This is a fine line to walk and learning to do so successfully is something that will only happen with practice which is why it is important to try to do as much practice as possible.

Consider scripting: Scripting is a useful means of getting started practicing being assertive if you aren't comfortable with the practice as it will allow you to figure out just what you were going to say in advance so there is little question as to what you will do next. In order to find the perfect thing to say you will want to start by focusing on the specific event that is taking place. This means you will want to break things down exactly how you see the problem as well as what you see the most likely solution to be.

From there, the next thing you are going to want to think about it is the way the situation currently makes you feel. This will make it easier for you to come to a decision when it comes to the best way to express your feelings while at the same time ensuring that your response isn't seen as a criticism or judgement of the other person. Keep in mind that making your feelings clear is the only way you can express to the other person how important that whatever you are requesting come to pass which is what you will be discussing when it comes to talking about your needs. This will also make it possible for you to guarantee that the person you are speaking with knows exactly where you are going from so that you can be confident that there are no misunderstandings between you.

This also leaves them free to choose a response that most clearly adheres to their response to your intended meaning. It is also important to clearly indicate what it is you want the results of your request to be, either the benefits that go along with your plan or the consequences of going against it. Choosing the right tactic is an important part of ensuring that your assertive plea is also persuasive.

Anger is acceptable: One of the most difficult things for many people to do when they are learning to become assertive is understand that expressing that you are angry is different than expressing yourself in an angry fashion. The truth of the matter is that anger doesn't have to be an inherently negative thing and it is sometimes a very natural response to a given situation. People who have a problem with anger have a problem expressing it in an effective may. If you can manage to express your anger is a way that is free of excessive negativity then it can be as healthy as any other emotion. Remember, understanding that all your feelings are valid is an important part of becoming assertive.

Ensure your requests are clear: When it comes to doing everything in your power to ensure that each of your assertive requests is met with an appropriate response, it is important to do what you can to ensure that those requests are done in a way that is both rational and clear. A request that is assertive in a positive way is one that is straight to the point while also taking clear steps to no make the other party feel inferior in any way. This is essentially the opposite of a passive-aggressive request which is often directly designed to hurt the recipient while also allowing the person who said it to hide behind a veil of innocence.

Validate your requests: In order to ensure you remain assertive rather than aggressive it is important to take an extra moment to always try and understand just where the other party is coming from. If you can understand the feelings that the other party is trying to express, then it becomes much easier for them to understand where you are coming from as well. This is not the same as agreeing with them, however, and should instead just do wonders when it comes to making them feel as though you are really listening which should, in theory, make it easier for you to get your way without being seen as aggressive.

When listening to what the other person has to say it is crucial that you do what you can to come across as respectful in both your verbal and nonverbal words and actions. This attitude of openness and respect can help the other person feel more relaxed and thus more likely to give in to your way of thinking. To help with this it is important to always retain eye contact and to truly listen to what the other party has to say if you truly hope to find the type of solution that is best for everyone.

Posture matters: It doesn't matter what it is you are trying to be assertive about, you are going to come off as more persuasive if you say it with your shoulders squared and your back straight. When you speak you are going to want to always look straight ahead which signals that you are always willing to face the reaction to the things you are saying. This will also show the person you are speaking with that you are willing to face their conversation head on while also looking for a reaction that is largely positive.

While working on the above it is also important that you work to look as relaxed as possible because there is nothing that will kill the positive vibes you have created like looking tense. Looking this way

Stephen Patterson

either means you are lying or are looking for a fight, neither or which is something that is likely to put another person in a good mood. Looking relaxed, on the other hand, also makes it easier for you to look confident, which will make it more likely the other party will go along with what you have to say as a result.

When you are speaking with another person directly you will also want to take steps to ensure your body is physically aligned with theirs as well. At the bare minimum, you should stand or sit, depending on what they are doing, though if you are standing then you will want to take the extra step of planting your feet at shoulder width to show the other party that you aren't hiding anything. What's more, this will also help you looked more relaxed and retain specific details more easily.

While you are talking to the other party you will find success if you try and slowly copy the gestures and mannerisms they use. This will serve to not only help them feel more at ease but will also help make it more likely that any assertive suggestions you make are received in a positive fashion. You will be able to tell that you have fully convinced them to think about things your way when you can stop mimicking their body movements and they start mimicking what you are doing instead.

Hands and arms: When it come to your arms and your hands, the most important thing to keep in mind is that you should only take an action if it looks natural. If you make the mistake of overthinking things then you will end up stifling their fluidity, leaving you with something that feels forced, awkward and of no good to anyone. Essentially what this means is that if you don't naturally gesture all that much regularly it is not something you need to force as a bad gesture is much worse than no gesture at all.

As it is with your posture, your goal with your arms and hands should be to look as relaxed as you can always. If you are being assertive about a reasonable request then you should have no reason to be nervous, after all. Above everything else, however, it is important that you never stand with your arms crossed unless you want to give off that very specific type of message. Standing in that way shows that you are disinterested in working towards a group consensus and only want things to be your way or the highway.

In order to be assertive in an appropriate way, you will want to stand so that your arms naturally hang by your side. This will indicate to those you are speaking with that you are looking to come to a real consensus which means listening to what others have to say as opposed to just getting your own way. You will want to avoid having balled fists while doing so, however, and if you are sitting you will want to avoid placing both of your palms facedown as well. Both these actions indicate that you don't like the current state of the conversation and that you are feeling angry.

Even if you do not express yourself using hand movements it is still important that you take the time to cultivate a quality handshake. A good handshake is a crucial part of making a good first impression which can then be capitalized on when it comes time to be assertive. The ideal handshake is one that is firm without being aggressive. Anything that is more over-the-top than that is only an indication that you are looking to dominate the other person which is not the message you really want to send in most instances. On the other hand, adopting a limp handshake will tell the other person that they are in control which can make it more difficult to get you way when being assertive in the long run.

Chapter 12:
Improve Your Ability to Set Goals Successfully

In order to ensure that you can plan effectively, you are going to want to start by choosing the right types of goals to make sure you find the type of success you are looking for. The best way to do this is to make sure that the goals you set are SMART goals and then set sub-goals based on the broad goals that you have decided upon.

Smart goals are specific: A goal which is specific is almost twice as likely to be accomplished than one which is general. A truly specific goals can answer a series of definite questions.

- Who will be involved in achieving the goal?

- What, specifically, is the goal being set to accomplish?

- Where will the completion of the goal take place?

- When will the goal realistically be completed by?

- Which requirements or constraints around the goal will make it challenging to complete?

- Why does the goal need accomplishing and what will the benefit of doing so be?

SMART goals are measurable: A goal which is measurable makes it easy to determine precise metrics for success, progress or failure. Keeping goals measurable will help you and your teamwork through them at a steady pace rather than in fits and starts. If you are having a hard time making your goals measurable, try considering how many or how much of something might indicate success or failure. Likewise, starting from the endpoint and working backwards may be easier, consider how you will know the goal has been successfully completed and then working towards the beginning can make measure goals easier

The best way to keep your goals measurable is to set up a generalized timetable based on whatever it is that you have planned for yourself and then keep track of how you are doing in relation to it. This timetable won't need to be extremely precise, if it has specific deadlines that you can always actively be working towards than it is doing its job. Keeping tabs on your success in chunks will ensure that you not only start off on the right foot but keep that success up all the way through to the finish line as well.

SMART goals are attainable: A good goal is one that is realistically attainable which means that you understand any potential roadblocks that may stand between you and the goal in question and that they will be ultimately surmountable. This means you are going to want to take a good hard look at your goal from all sides and be realistic with yourself about your chances for success. While looking at your goal through rose colored glasses might make you feel better, it is truly in your best interest to be as critical during this step as possible.

The trick here is to pick a goal that is attainable enough to keep you working diligently at it, while not so easy that it wouldn't make sense to have sub-goals surrounding completing it successfully. While 20 years out might be a bit excessive for your current needs, everyone can benefit from a good five-year plan. If you land on a goal that is either too difficult to achieve or too easy to warrant striving towards you will find it much for difficult to work to achieve it successfully.

SMART goals are realistic: A good goal is one that is realistic in addition to being attainable which means that you can expect success without something extremely unlikely being required to push reality into your favor. An ideal goal is one that is going to require a good amount of work to achieve, while remaining not so difficult as to become unrealistic. Additionally, you are going to want to shy away from goals that you can meet without putting for any real amount of effort as goals that are too easy can actually be demotivating as it then becomes easy to continue putting them off and putting them off until they eventually fade into oblivion.

SMART goals are timely: A good goal is one that as a clear timetable for when it is going to be completed. Even the best-intentioned goals are likely to fall apart if their timetable is to strict, but also if it is too generous. Timetables that are too condensed increase the odds of requiring you too cut corners in order to find success while those that are too long can be beset by unexpected complications that would have been avoided had the timetable been a little shorter. Finding the right timeframe is key to keeping your motivation levels at the right point to ensure success in a reasonable period.

What this means is that you will want to determine what your goal will be, determine a timeline for completion, and then do the same for each of the sub-goals you set as well. When it comes to setting a due date for your goals, you will want to consider periods of time that are long enough to allow you to realistically experience a few setbacks along the way, without being so lax that you never actually get around to accomplishing anything. What you are shooting for is something that will force you to stop dreaming about financial freedom and start working towards it, not something so strict that you have no realistic chance of success.

Determining assumptions and constraints: After you have an objective in place, the next thing you will need to include will be the constraints and assumptions as the three together will provide you with the general scope you are looking to do.

When it comes to determining assumptions, you will want to make a list of all the things that you are going to assume to be true when it comes to the planning stage. This includes things like being able to acquire the resources you need to complete the goal and find people who can help you as required. You will also want to make assumptions when it comes to the length of time each stage of the project will take, that other projects will finish on time, etc.

When listing out your assumptions, it is important to be realistic as well. This means you can assume you will have the time to complete your goal, but not that you will have so much time to devote to it that you can expect it to get done more quickly than average. Listing out your assumptions can be a slippery slope, simply because it can be easy to lose the line between what you know will happen and what you want to happen, so it is important to remain vigilant. If any of your assumptions aren't 100 percent guaranteed to come to pass, then you will want to ensure you have a backup plan in place as well to ensure you don't end up wasting any time.

Stephen Patterson

When making your list of constraints, you are only going to want to list out those things that you know, for a fact, that you are going to have to work around. While you may find that constraints make the goal more complicated to achieve having a clear idea of what you are up against right from the start will only help to make things simpler in the long-term.

Implementation: After your SMART Goals have been decided upon, it is a good idea to try and generalize all the goals into five primary ones which can be easily focused on. The fewer the number of goals the more likely they will be acted upon in a reasonable frame of time. If goals cannot be easily generalized, it is important to instead start with the ones that will make the most difference and then work down the list from there. Regardless of what you settle on, it is important to ensure each goal has a means for easily keeping track of its progress.

Decide on tactics: For each goal, you will want to consider how it can best be completed by slotting it into your current schedule. This process should include enough consideration to ensure that tactics and goals align. Tactics are likely to change as the goal heads towards success and should be studied to ensure they remain appropriate for the goal in question.

Act: After tactics have been decided upon, it is time to put them into practice. This is the stage where the rubber hits the road, quality goals should always require total buy-in to be their most successful.

Review as needed: Once the action is in progress it is important to monitor and change the action as needed. The best goals are constantly being improved and your goals and the implementation thereof should be no exception.

Understand the difference between ambition and goals: When you first begin working to improve the quality of the goals you set it is important to frame your goals in a realistic manner. As previously stated, the human mind works best when it can link effort with the reward which means setting yourself up with an unreasonable ambition is a recipe for disaster. As such it is important that you have both general ambitions about the skill plus specific goals that you can meet on a regular basis. For example, learning to speak French fluently is an ambition, which if it is your only goal will cause you to give up long before you obtain it. However, if you instead make it your goal to learn 100 new French words every week, that is a goal which can be objectively accomplished in a reasonable period.

Try the 80/20 principle: Also known as the Pareto principle, the 80/20 principle is a simple ratio that explains the idea that 80

Stephen Patterson

percent of your results come from 20 percent of your effort. This is a common refrain among sales teams but is equally true of many languages, including English. 20 percent of the words are repeated 80 percent of the time; it is the same with pop music. This principle can be applied to learning if you first take the time to understand with reasonable surety what the most important 20 percent of a topic is. Again, it is important to only apply this principal when you can be more than 75 percent sure you understand what the most important 20 percent of a topic to be. Remember, a little knowledge is a dangerous thing.

Conclusion

Just because you've finished this book doesn't mean there is nothing left to learn on the topic, and expanding your horizons is the only way to find the mastery you seek.

With so many different aspects of your mindset to work on, it can be tempted to start on all of them at once. This is only likely to lead to failure, however, which is why it is a far better choice to start with the aspect of the mental toughness mindset that is most important to you, or the one that seems as though it will have the greatest immediate benefit in your life instead. Doing so will give you the single-minded focus to not only learn to access that aspect of the mindset but to master it as well.

What's more, it is important to keep in mind that while the means of doing so are relatively straightforward, changing even the simplest aspect of your mindset is going to take plenty of hard work and determination if you want it to stick. As such, it can be thought of like a marathon rather than a sprint which means that slow and steady will win the race every time.

Stephen Patterson

If you find this book helpful in anyway a review to support my endeavors is much appreciated.

www.ingramcontent.com/pod-product-compliance
Lightning Source LLC
Chambersburg PA
CBHW020403080526
44584CB00014B/1154